New Foreword by Fath.

Prayer &
Temperament

Different Prayer Forms
For Different Personality Types

Chester P. Michael • *Marie C. Norrisey*

Published by Open Door Inc.
opendoorsdi.org

Cover design by Kenneth Wilfong, mtn laurel studio
Interior design by Rachel L. Hall, Writely Divided

ISBN 978-1-7379089-0-6

Library of Congress Control Number: 84-61839

Prayer and Temperament: Different Prayer Forms for Different Personality Types / Chester P. Michael and Marie C. Norrisey — 3rd ed.

In grateful acknowledgment to all those who participated in the 1982 Prayer Project.

Without their enthusiastic support, this project could not have been undertaken.

CONTENTS

FOREWORD

I cannot claim to have known Monsignor Chester Michael in any depth but I was fortunate enough to have met him toward the end of his life. On a couple of occasions, I was able to listen to his teaching and enjoy some informal conversation with him. I found him an unpretentious man, confident in his knowledge and experience, concise and clear in his teaching, unapologetically direct and directive. As he answered questions, I was struck that his replies were not abstract, but tailored to the personality of the individual he addressed. He seemed to understand that one size would *not* fit all.

My familiarity with *Prayer and Temperament*, the book he co-authored with the late Marie Norrisey, has made Father Chet a three-dimensional character for me. And I have had ample opportunity to meet many of the people he directed or shaped as spiritual directors through the Spiritual Direction Institute (SDI) which he founded. Even more than Chet's writing, this living legacy and the personal recollections I have enjoyed hearing make him a living presence.

Prayer and Temperament has been a great help to me, both when I was novice director at Holy Cross Abbey and now as guest master at our retreat house. I have lent out copies of the book many times and it is usually a challenge to get them back! This is a helpful and valuable book.

Personality Type and Prayer

Too often in our pragmatic, production-oriented, American culture, formation to prayer is reduced to techniques. Prayer is not just another artifact, destined for the mantelpiece, nor is it a label establishing my identity. I like to describe prayer as my relationship with God—and I prefer to share this concrete description to an abstract definition when exploring prayer with another person. Each relationship is unique and unrepeatable, fed by the ups and downs, working out the misunderstandings, as well as thriving from understanding and communion. Each member of the relationship brings their experience and personhood to the mix. A few pointers may be helpful, but techniques are not sufficiently organic or flexible to provide the give-and-take feeding a vital relationship requires. This book, *Prayer and Temperament*, should not be read like an operator's manual, but as a portal framing lived experience.

This is also not the place to explore the intimate connection between psychological development and spirituality—that is not the task of this book. But it is as good a place as any to admit how many of us, like Fr. Chet himself during his seminary years, were corralled into one approach to prayer, presented as the only correct way to pray. In his day, it was what he names the Thomistic form of prayer. When I was a novice, that style was out of fashion, and we were taught that any conceptual approach to prayer, any imagery or affect, even verbal expressions, were to be rejected to arrive at pure prayer. Anything else was considered a compromise resulting from the beginner's ineptitude.

Any exclusive technique or approach to prayer, ignoring the personality profile of the individual, leaves the neophyte feeling inferior and frustrated. What has been described as "happening" in that so-called ideal of prayer may never be experienced; whereas, healthy, native tendencies will be taken as "distractions" rather than appropriate resources.

The unfortunate result is that it is easier to flee prayer or, just as bad, dutifully sacrifice time to lifeless, disengaged prayer, either option leaving the individual spiritually undernourished, or even depleted.

Perhaps this is why I so often hear that some parish priests are unwilling to provide spiritual direction: what they were taught merely frustrated them, convincing them that they have nothing to offer. The alternative of prescribed rituals or vocal prayers may not speak to everyone, degenerating into robotic exercises, a checklist completed to appease a bookkeeping deity.

Persona and Shadow

Spirituality and prayer cannot be detached from real life or psychological development. If we spend the early years of adulthood establishing our *persona*—our public face and role in society—constructing its proper boundaries and positive capacities, at midlife we are faced with the realization that we are hardly identical with our carefully buffed persona.

Of course, I certainly need a public face to function in society. When I don my Cistercian habit, I assume an identity which allows strangers to trust and confide in me, to expect a certain level of competence, expertise, credibility and trust. God forbid if I violate those expectations and boundaries! But God forbid if I actually believe that I am nothing but my persona.

Whereas no one should have to suffer my pettiness, my prejudices, my insecurities, my dishonesty, I cannot simply hide them. I can never afford to ignore them or fail to take responsibility for them. Anything that has no place in my persona is part of my shadow, which, if ignored or denied, will pop out in my interactions with others, despite my best intentions.

A valuable contribution of *Prayer and Temperament* is to help the reader identify both their psychological profile and the shadow it casts. The deficits, as well as the assets, of each type are also delineated here, so none of us can assume that where we find ourselves is in any way superior. Nor is it a point of arrival; it is not good enough in itself but as a point of departure for further growth. That can be an enormous help to relieve prayer of the false burden of perfectionism or refining some "finished product." There is no product. There is—and is not this much better?—an on-going relationship.

The third edition's Chapter Eight, "Using our Shadow and Inferior Function in Prayer," is an improvement over the original. The editors of this anniversary edition realized that clarification was needed, and I believe this is a timely intervention.

We live in a polarized world, evident in our churches, our political life, our social media, our public interchanges. It is not unlike the delicate balance of contrary forces and conflicting "isms" that C. G. Jung struggled to understand and address from after

World War I through the Cold War. Now as then, individuals and nations are not owning and shepherding their shadow side but unconsciously projecting it on "the other." This irresponsibility is a strategy for disaster, and we see the collateral damage not only on our relationships, our institutions and in individual lives but on the natural environment. Now as then, we need more and more people to recognize and work with the shadow if we are to ever find our common ground as creative communities. Without that, there can be no real community, only partisan divisions, opposing camps, reducing our planet to a battle field.

An open-minded reading of this book could be a contribution to our collective, not just our personal, growth. Reading the whole book—and not just what applies to me—will certainly help me appreciate others.

As I work on my shadow, my profile will shift. Like any relationship, my prayer will change over time and I will incorporate aspects helpful to the prayer of other personality types. I can never complacently presume that I know how to pray and settle into a comfortable routine. It is one of the great—if largely interior—adventures in life.

Spiritual Direction

Anyone who has had the privileged responsibility of spiritual direction, or accompaniment, realizes that it is not a one-way street. The director is not the dispenser of classified information to be doled out to the directee at the appropriate time. As I have mentioned above, this is not a technology. Like any pedagogy, this is an experimental and experiential art, a craft which is a dialogue between the "raw material" and the "artisan." In this particular art, however, the "director" and the "directee" are both artisan and raw material. The "director," too, is seeking and learning, filled with questions, deep listening and prayer, collaborating with the "directee," as they craft a rapport between each other and with God. One remains committed to this exacting art because of the growth generated by the interchange in both participants.

I find that dimension is well reflected in this present edition. The editors have benefitted for 30 years of using this book to refine its present shape as a teaching tool in the SDI and especially as basis for retreats, as included in the Appendices.

Particularly valuable for further study are the endnotes, absent from the original text.

—————

May the good work which has been begun by the preparation of this edition, be brought to completion in the coming of God's Kingdom.

Fr. James Orthmann, OCSO
Holy Cross Abbey
Berryville, Virginia
Feast of the Transfiguration
6 August 2021

INTRODUCTION TO THE
30ᵀᴴ ANNIVERSARY EDITION

What is the value in knowing ourselves? Monsignor Chester Michael, affectionately known as Father Chet, believed it was a key to spiritual growth and that the Myers-Briggs Type Indicator (MBTI) was a useful tool in helping us along the path. He saw its application in three ways:

- Love of God – knowledge of the MBTI as an aid to prayer facilitates relationship with God.
- Love of neighbor – MBTI can help us appreciate the differences between ourselves and others and realize that typological differences are neither wrong nor right, just differences.
- Healthy love of self – knowledge of our type can increase self-awareness and may heal old wounds resulting from criticisms of our differences from family and others.

While we know that MBTI has its critics,[1] that some prefer the ancient Enneagram or other tools such as the Big Five, the MBTI, and its underlying Jungian theory, remains resilient. What we also know is that in the 30 years since *Prayer and Temperament* was published, a preference-guided approach to prayer continues to resonate with individuals who are seeking to deepen their spiritual development. We base this on our own experiences as well as knowing that this book has been used by countless others in classes, workshops and retreats, prayer groups, formation for deacons, and by spiritual directors with directees.

This would not be a surprise to Father Chet and his co-author Marie Norrisey. As they wrote in the epilogue of the original edition, "Requests for more information on the topic arrive from far and near almost every day; therefore, in view of this demand, and the almost complete absence of published material on the subject, we felt called to publish this present book."

The roots of their work are traced to 1953, when Father Chet, who was a parish priest in the Diocese of Richmond, Virginia, began taking summer courses at Notre Dame. There he met and studied under the Jungian psychologist, Father Josef Goldbrunner. Father Goldbrunner was among the pioneers who saw the value of psychology in the training of priests, and its importance to spiritual health in general; his ideas were brought forth in his seminal lecture "In Holiness is Wholeness."[2] Father Chet became heavily influenced by both the writings of Carl Jung and Pierre Teilhard de Chardin. Episcopal priest and Notre Dame instructor Morton Kelsey, author of over 30 books on spiritual development and also a correspondent with Jung, introduced Father to the MBTI in 1976.

With a growing understanding and interest in cognitive preferences, Father began considering human temperament and its possible connection or influence upon spirituality and prayer. It was Marie's suggestion to launch the Prayer Project to determine on a large scale if there was any connection between MBTI and prayer (see Appendix II). The project was a significant undertaking for Father and Marie, who volunteered her keen administrative capabilities. While it was a large study, it was nonrandomized: a majority of participants were women and there was a preponderance of religious and clergy compared to laypeople. Yet the experience so resonated with those who participated, that Father and Marie wanted to offer their findings and conclusions to a wider audience and thus published this book.

It was their hope that *Prayer and Temperament* would spark others to study and write in this area, yet that has largely not happened. As a result, The Open Door board decided to republish the text confirming its accuracy regarding temperament theories, checking and updating source material to create endnotes that include information from the first edition and new material as needed, consolidating the original appendices into the main body of the book which provides for a more robust discussion especially on using the shadow and inferior functions, refreshing some language and correcting mistakes, and providing a new appendix on how to organize a retreat using the text. We feel these changes were ones Father and Marie would have also made if they were still with us.

When asked during an interview in 2004 as what was the most satisfying part of his ministry, Father Chet, who at that point had served as a priest for 62 years, responded that it was spiritual direction.[3] That is what *Prayer and Temperament* continues to offer today. The gift of Father and Marie through this book still encourages, guides, advises, confronts and challenges each of us on our path toward holiness.

Editors
30th Anniversary Edition
July 2021
opendoorsdi.org

INTRODUCTION

During the past several decades with its emphasis on personal growth and fulfillment, a good amount of interest has been generated concerning the relationship between one's temperament or personality and one's style of prayer and spirituality. During many workshops, seminars, retreat experiences, and in the spiritual direction of numerous persons, the authors experimented with the theory that there is a relationship between one's temperament and the kind of prayer or spirituality that is practiced by different persons.

The origin of this book started in 1982 by recruiting people from all over the country to engage in a year-long project to discern the value of various prayer forms for the different psychological types of human personality. Of those 415 individuals who took part in the project, 98 percent testified to the value of choosing a method of prayer which was compatible to their temperament.

Everyone involved in the Prayer Project took either the Myers-Briggs Type Indicator (MBTI),[1] the quicker Keirsey-Bates Temperament Sorter,[2] or the Gray-Wheelwright Jungian Type Survey,[3] which is especially helpful for discerning one's Dominant and Inferior Functions. The method used by the various personality tests to determine one's type[4] is to ask a series of questions to determine preferences of how one views and perceives reality and how one acts and makes judgments.

People who have taken either the Myers-Briggs Type Indicator (MBTI) or the shorter Keirsey Temperament Sorter attest to the accuracy with which the portraits describe the temperament and personality of the individual. It almost appears as though someone has been following each of us around and is describing our own individual personality instead of giving a general description of one of sixteen types of personality. These indicators so accurately describe one's characteristic or habitual inclination that we strongly recommend that each person in a relationship, family or otherwise, and every member of a staff or working group should take the MBTI and share the findings with the other members of their group. Such sharing would probably eliminate much of the misunderstandings which normally arise in close relationships or working groups. Not only will we understand ourselves better and why we perceive reality and make judgments and decisions the way we do, but we will also understand why others see reality differently and arrive at decisions at variance with our own. General knowledge of the differences in human temperament should help to overcome much intolerance and many misunderstandings in human society.

In addition to the wonderful benefits of self-understanding and mutual understanding in personal, community, religious, and work groupings, many of us have discovered another tremendous benefit from knowing something about type and temperament. We are realizing that there is a different type of prayer and spirituality that is appropriate to each of the four basic temperaments and perhaps also even for the sixteen different types of personality.

The research of Briggs-Myers and Keirsey-Bates was done in the secular fields. So far little extensive research has been done in the application of these findings to prayer and spirituality.[5] However, as a result of the study, and our personal experience, certain conclusions concerning methods of prayer for the different types and temperaments have emerged. Those who have followed the suggestions offered by us during the Prayer Project and in spiritual direction have found real help in developing a more meaningful prayer life which in turn spurs on their spiritual growth.

One of the great tragedies during the past several centuries is that we have been more or less forced by training into a form of prayer or spirituality that is actually a proper method for a particular temperament. Unfortunately, that temperament belonged to only a small number of those who took seriously the need for prayer. One was given the impression that this traditional method of prayer was the best method for everyone. When a person did not feel fulfilled, the conclusion was that there was something wrong with the person rather than with the method. Therefore, many of us decided that we were not destined for sanctity since the recommended way of spirituality could not be achieved, even with supreme and heroic effort. The result was that many good people gave up prayer altogether or went through the motions of praying without any real interior effect or benefit.

In our 1982 survey of the relationship between temperament and prayer, there were participants in all sixteen of the individual types of human personality. Of the 415 people surveyed, 300 of the participants were women and 115 were men. Of these, 44 were clergymen of various church affiliations, 84 were women of different religious communities, and 287 were lay persons. Throughout the year regular reports of their reactions to the different prayer suggestions and other material, which we sent them, were returned to us. With the help of the criticisms and suggestions given by the participants, we corrected any inaccuracies that had existed in our theories concerning the relationship between temperament and particular forms of prayer. It is also worthy to acknowledge that while the initial study was skewed to religious, our practical experience over the years concludes that these findings are widely applicable to the general population.

Adapting the findings of the MBTI to the amelioration of our spiritual life is one of a number of tools which can help us in our growth toward wholeness and holiness.[6] Like any tool, however, it is not universally applicable. There will be a number of persons who do not fit into the molds suggested by the four basic temperaments and the sixteen personality types. This is typical of the human situation where every person is unique and somewhat different from every other human being.

We are also not saying that you knowing your temperament is required to grow in spirituality. Those who are able to pray without the benefit of a knowledge of temperament should continue to follow the path that works best for them. What we are saying is that based on our experience, a very large majority, if not nearly all, of those who are introduced to the theory of temperament or type do find that this knowledge becomes an excellent tool to help them pray better. By learning their type with its good attributes and shortcomings, they have been helped to understand their strengths and limitations and how to use in prayer those parts of their personality which do not function naturally or easily.

Everything written in this book about the relationship of temperament and prayer needs to be taken with certain reservations. The conclusions drawn are never to be taken absolutely. They are only somewhat true and somewhat applicable. The rule to follow is to try out the suggestions. If they work for you and help deepen your prayer life and your relationship with God, then make use of them.

Since most persons who have tried to follow these suggestions have found them helpful to their prayer life, the hope is that you, too, will experience some benefit from them. Think of them as "tools" that are meant to assist your efforts to connect with God, to maintain this relationship, and to deepen it through your prayer.

God can and frequently does directly intervene in our lives in His own way. We must keep ourselves open to whatever helps we can get from every possible source. The study and knowledge of temperament and type is one of these helps.

Msgr. Michael and Marie Norrisey
1991

Prayer &
Temperament

CHAPTER ONE

An Overview

THE HISTORY & DEVELOPMENT OF THE
THEORY OF TEMPERAMENT

For at least twenty-five centuries, human beings have been aware of certain distinct differences in human temperament or personality. Around 450 B.C., Hippocrates, the Father of Medical Science, divided the human race into four temperaments. His theory was that the cause of the differences in human personality was an imbalance of the four "humors" or secretions of the heart, liver, lungs, and kidneys. He designated the temperaments according to these four secretions: sanguine (blood from the heart); choleric (bile from the liver); phlegmatic (phlegm from the lungs); and melancholic (bile from the kidneys). Galen, a great Greco-Roman physician, took up the theory of Hippocrates and amplified it by showing that differences of temperament were something positive rather than a negative imbalance of bodily secretions. In the sixteenth century a Swiss physician, theologian, and alchemist named Paracelsus further elaborated the theory of four basic temperaments by using the four elements of water, earth, air, and fire to distinguish their different traits.

The division of human personalities into four basic temperaments continued to be the traditional theory until Carl G. Jung published his study of personality types in 1920.[1] By positing two attitudes toward life (Extraversion and Introversion) and four operating functions (Sensation, Intuition, Thinking, Feeling), Jung arrived at a total of eight different psychological types. In this country Katharine C. Briggs and her daughter, Isabel Briggs Myers, took up the findings of Jung and after forty years of research and amplification came out in 1962 with the Myers-Briggs Type Indicator through which sixteen types of personality could be distinguished. After her mother's death and all through her life, Isabel Briggs Myers continued her work with human temperament; and her findings and conclusions were published in *Gifts Differing in 1980*,[2] co-written with her son, just before her death.

Meanwhile, David Keirsey, a clinical psychologist working in California, further expanded on the insights of Jung and the MyersBriggs team, and with Marilyn Bates published *Please Understand Me* in 1976.[3] From the sixteen types of personality identified by Isabel Myers, Keirsey isolated four basic temperaments of human behavior. Each of these four temperaments has four subtypes following the sixteen types demarcated in Myers-Briggs.

The Four Pairs of Preferences

E-I   S-N   T-F   J-P

Both the Briggs-Myers team and the Keirsey-Bates team use four pairs of preferences—Extraversion-Introversion, Sensing-

Intuition, Thinking-Feeling, Judging-Perceiving – to arrive at the sixteen distinct types of human personality. Two of these pairs of preferences (E-I and J-P) are termed attitudes, while the other two pairs (S-N and T-F) are called functions. Briggs Myers assigned letters to each of these eight choices: E for Extraversion, I for Introversion, S for Sensing, N for Intuition, T for Thinking, F for Feeling, J for Judging, and P for Perceiving. The MBTI gives the relative strength of each person's preference.[4]

According to the temperament theory of Jung and Briggs Myers, everyone has some ability in all of the choices, but most people show a marked tendency to use one side of each of the four pairs of preferences and neglect to use the other side except when necessary.[5] This results in a more or less habitual use of one side of each pair of preferences in all our conscious behavior and conscious life and the relegation of the opposite side to the realm of the unconscious.[6] This opposite side is called an inferior function or attitude or sometimes one's shadow.[7] This attribute is available for use in our conscious life but requires considerably more psychic energy[8] to activate than does the conscious habitually-used side. The sixteen types, designated by the particular four letters which comprise our habitual, conscious choices in the four pairs of preferences, are: ESTJ, ISTJ, ESTP, ISTP, ESFJ, ISFJ, ESFP, ISFP, ENTJ, INTJ, ENTP, INTP, ENFJ, INFJ, ENFP, INFP.

The first pair of preferences (E-I) conveys how one tends to relate with the world. The Extravert relies primarily on the outer world of people and things to receive the needed psychic energy and enthusiasm for living. The Introvert relies primarily upon the inner world of ideas, concepts, and spirit in order to find the needed energy to live. Every human being can be extraverted or introverted depending upon the occasion, but most people definitely prefer to be one more than the other.

The second and third pairs of preferences (S-N, T-F) refer to the four basic psychological functions which everyone uses for perceiving new data and in making the necessary judgment or decision for acting upon this data. The Perceiving Functions, Sensing and Intuition, are the second pair of preferences; and the Judging Functions, Thinking and Feeling, the third pair of preferences.

The Perceiving Functions, Sensing and Intuition, are used to gather the data and information which we use in order to carry on our life. Sensing makes use of the five bodily senses of seeing, hearing, touching, tasting, and smelling to contact the actual state of affairs as it exists in the here and now. The Sensing Function is primarily concerned with gathering data of the physical world in which we live, including our own body and all outside, physical, material bodies. In general, the Sensing Function furnishes us with the data of the actual situation in which we presently find ourselves. Yet, by means of symbols, the Sensing Function is also able to connect with the inner world of spirit. For example, it tells us whether we are happy or sad, enthusiastic or depressed, peaceful or disturbed. Through a symbol-making process, the Sensing Function senses the presence of God and the transcendental level of reality as distinct from the physical world.

The Intuitive Function perceives the great potential and new possibilities in both the external physical world and the inner world of spirit and ideas. As the creative, visionary function, Intuition makes it possible for us to create new things or bring about improvements in the present situation. While the Sensing

Function is primarily concerned with the external physical world and only secondarily involved with the inner world of spirit, the Intuitive Function is primarily concerned with the inner world and only secondarily concerned with the outer world. Thus, the two Perceiving Functions are complementary, and both are needed for a full and balanced life. However, depending upon individual temperament, each of us tends to favor one way of perceiving rather than the other.

The two Judging Functions, Thinking and Feeling, are used to make the necessary judgments and decisions as to what we will do with the data which has been furnished by the Perceiving Functions. Both make value judgments but arrive at them through different methods. The Thinking Function uses the mind and intellect to arrive at a judgment or decision by following a logical, methodical method. The Feeling Function uses the heart and inner experiences of personal relationship and love to arrive at its judgment and decision. The Thinking Function is more objective and impersonal, emphasizing justice, objective truth, fairness. The Feeling Function is more subjective and personal, emphasizing the personal values and the effects which the decision or judgment will have on the persons involved, whether they be oneself or others. In making good judgments and decisions, we need to use both the Thinking Function and the Feeling Function, but each of us is inclined to give more weight to one function rather than to the other, making it one of the four determining factors of our temperament or personality.

Of these four functions – Sensing, Intuition, Thinking, Feeling – one will be the Dominant Function upon which a person relies more heavily than any of the others. The opposite of the Dominant Function is called the Inferior Function because it is undifferentiated and more or less deeply buried in the unconscious. Another function is called the Auxiliary Function because it is the main help upon which the Dominant Function relies to carry out its particular work. The opposite of the Auxiliary Function is simply called the third or Tertiary Function. For example, if the Dominant is a Perceiving Function (Sensing or Intuition), then the Auxiliary will always be a Judging Function (Thinking or Feeling). Vice-versa is also true: If the Dominant Function is a Judging Function, the Auxiliary will always be a Perceiving Function. In the order of ascendancy, then, it would be Dominant, Auxiliary, Tertiary, and Inferior.

In her study of human personalities Isabel Myers discovered an interesting phenomenon. Extraverts use their Dominant Function when dealing with the external world and rely on their Auxiliary Function when dealing with the inner world of ideas, concepts, spirit. On the other hand, Introverts use their Dominant Function in the inner world, and depend upon their Auxiliary Function when they deal with the external world. For this reason, Introverts are much more difficult to get to know. Since they do not show their Dominant Function to the external world but show their Auxiliary, it is difficult to type their temperament accurately.

Myers and Briggs also discovered that each one of us shows a definite preference for using either the Perceiving Functions or the Judging Functions when relating to the world. Therefore, they added a fourth pair of preferences and called them Judging and Perceiving. Those who prefer using the Judging Functions, Thinking and Feeling, when relating to the world around them, are called the "J" people. They give their main attention and concern to making judgments and decisions about how things and persons in the world should act. Those who prefer using their Perceiving Functions, Sensing and Intuition, in relating to the outside world are called "P" people. They are primarily concerned with getting more data and information without coming to closure. The "J" persons are quite structured and decisive in their approach to life. The "P" persons are usually more flexible and open-ended. They usually are slower in arriving at a decision than the "J" people. The "P" person is less structured and less time-conscious than the "J" person.

Function Theory versus Temperament Theory

Isabel Myers and those who have followed her lead are primarily concerned about the relationship of the different functions in regard to temperament. David Keirsey, while acknowledging the value and place of the functions in determining temperament, has sought to bring the insights of Jung and Briggs-Myers into accord with the very ancient and constant tradition of four basic temperaments. To do this he has been concerned more with the external behavior of the different types rather than how each type functions. Thus, he has arrived at a theory of four basic temperaments: Sensing Judging (SJ), Sensing-Perceiving (SP), Intuition-Thinking (NT), and Intuition-Feeling (NF). Note that in this classification, Keirsey uses only two pairs of preferences in determining the basic temperament. When the Perceiving Function is Sensing, he uses the fourth pair of preferences, J or P. When the Perceiving Function is Intuition, he uses the third pair of preferences, T or F. Arriving at this conclusion by the inductive method of studying the four typical pathological cases of hysteria, depression, compulsion, and impulsive behavior, he then discovered that the behavior of normal, healthy people also fell into these same four categories or temperaments.

The two opinions seem to arise from different points of view with which we can approach human personality. If we approach it from the aspect of outward behavior, then the use of the four basic temperaments described by Keirsey and Bates is quite accurate. If we approach it from the angle of how the inner functions operate, then the descriptions of temperaments and types of personality given by Isabel Briggs Myers seems to fit the situation best. It is not a case of either/or but of both/and. In this book, we have attempted to use the insights of both Myers and Keirsey. To do so, we have made a distinction between spirituality and prayer. Spirituality concerns our behavior in the three basic relationships: with God, with our neighbor, and with ourselves. Prayer concerns the inner workings of the specific relationship with God.

Keirsey cites four Greek gods for their attributes and names them as the patrons of these four basic temperaments: Epimethean (SJ), Dionysian (SP), Promethean (NT), and Apollonian (NF).[9] These four basic temperaments resemble somewhat the four temperaments of Hippocrates. SJ might also be termed Melancholic; SP Sanguine; NT-Phlegmatic; NF-Choleric. In this book, we have used the names of four well-known saints to identify these four temperaments and their appropriate spirituality. We have called the SJ temperament and spirituality Ignatian (St. Ignatius of Loyola); the SP, Franciscan (St. Francis of Assisi); the NT, Thomistic (St. Thomas Aquinas); and the NF, Augustinian (St. Augustine of Hippo).

Relationship of Temperament to Prayer and Spirituality

All indicators point to a close relationship between our innate temperament and the type of prayer best suited to our needs. Introverts will prefer a form of prayer different from Extraverts. Intuitives approach God from a point of view different from Sensers. Feelers pray in a different way from Thinkers. Judging persons want structure in their prayer life, while Perceiving persons want flexibility. As we grow in maturity and learn to make good use of all our abilities in functioning and relating, our prayer life should become richer. While we may still prefer the type of prayer that matches our natural temperament, we should familiarize ourselves with the other forms of prayer that have been developed over the centuries.

As far as the relation of prayer to the four functions is concerned, our recommendation is that, for the most part, we should use our Dominant and Auxiliary Functions in our daily prayer periods. Since we have the most facility with these two functions, prayer will not become a burden if we rely primarily upon them; but we should also try to use our Tertiary Function frequently. The Inferior Function should not be entirely neglected in prayer since, according to Jung, this is the function which the unconscious uses most often to reveal the riches of the inner life of the spirit. Using this fourth, undeveloped function requires much more psychic energy than does using the Dominant and Auxiliary Functions. Therefore, it would be a mistake to attempt to activate this inferiorly developed function in all of our prayer periods. For most people, if this were attempted, prayer would become too much of a burden and most likely would be abandoned. Rather, we should wait for those more leisurely moments in our life when we have lots of time to muster the extra psychic energy needed to use the Inferior Function. If used then, some of the deepest and most meaningful faith experiences may occur. The Tertiary Function acts somewhat after the manner of the Inferior Function and somewhat after the manner of the Auxiliary Function. Therefore, it can be activated with less effort than the Inferior Function but still not as easily as the Auxiliary or Dominant Functions. This is more fully elaborated in Chapter Nine.)

We are able to contact God and experience grace through all four of the psychological functions. Each of these functions has a transcendent dimension which enables us to get in touch with God and the spiritual, transcendental values of life. Some examples of these transcendentals are love, truth, beauty, goodness, unity, justice, life, adoration, worship, reverence, gratitude, and contrition. These are the values which we try to actualize in prayer and through prayer energize in our conscious life. Through the activation of the transcendent dimension of each of the four functions we receive the psychic energy necessary to perform our daily duties, connect with God in prayer, discern God 's will, and receive the grace to fulfill our destiny on earth. (See Chapter Eight for a further explanation of the transcendent dimension and its relationship to the shadow and prayer.)

Prayer touches and influences us only to the extent that it succeeds in activating the transcendent dimension of one or more of the four functions of Sensing, Intuition, Thinking, and Feeling. The different prayer forms described in this book will enable one to energize the transcendent dimension of the different functions. Our recommendation is that one should use all five of the methods described in order to vitalize all four functions and thus create a proper balance in our ordinary life, in our prayer life, and in our relationship with God. By practicing all five of the methods of prayer described, one will discover the particular method or methods that best fit one's temperament and personality.

Normally, this will be the prayer form that emphasizes the use of our Dominant and Auxiliary Functions. This then would be our "bread and butter" prayer, which can be used most of the time, for example, three or four days of every week. But we should also expose ourselves, perhaps once a week, to each of the other forms of prayer. In this way we will learn to activate the transcendent dimension of all four functions. Perhaps on the weekend, when we have more time and leisure for prayer and are under less pressure from work, we could use the extra time and psychic energy to energize and use our Inferior and Tertiary Functions in prayer. If so, one may be surprised to discover that these will be the prayer times when our deepest and most beautiful experiences of God's love, power, goodness, mercy, wisdom, and presence will occur.

Just as we have Dominant and Inferior Functions, so also do we have a dominant temperament (NF, NT, SJ, SP), while its opposite is our inferior temperament. The other two basic temperaments will fall into the categories of auxiliary and tertiary temperaments. Jung always insisted that there is a polar balance between our conscious life and our unconscious. When one function or temperament is predominant in conscious activities, its opposite will be operating in unconscious areas of our life. Since many of our most intense experiences of God and grace rise out of our unconscious inner being, it behooves us not to neglect those types of prayer which require us to activate our inferior functions and inferior temperaments.

Shifts in Temperament and Methods of Prayer

Preferences with regard to attitudes and functions are established at a relatively young age and remain over the course of the lifespan.[10] However, it is also true that one's facility with regard to all the functions and attitudes can be strengthened through purposeful or imposed practice and usage. The analogy often used to explain how this occurs is the relationship between the right and left hand in how most favor one or the other. Lack of usage of the non-preferred hand renders it relatively weak and awkward in performing routine tasks independently. Training, as with the case of an accomplished pianist, allows use of either hand with near equal facility. So it is with the functions and attitudes; as you age and mature, one can develop different facets of their personality type.

Enhanced facility with the less dominant functions and attitudes can occur deliberately when someone becomes convinced of the value and need of change in outlook or behavior in order to satisfy one's self-esteem or to fulfill one's destiny. For others, the changes may be induced naturally over time, or due to life, and in particular, work requirements. Even if an individual does not try to strengthen the less preferred attitudes and functions, there is a natural tendency to gravitate toward their implementation and development, particularly at the stage of midlife.[11] It is also true that the modern, western business environment typically favors thinking over feeling, sensing over intuition, judging over perceiving, and extraversion over introversion. This phenomenon is a source of frequent confusion regarding type preference. Parental, family, peer, and cultural influences may also play a role, which calls to mind the story of the mother who famously announced to her friend, "My daughter is most certainly not an introvert. She is a perfectly lovely person!"

As we become more mature and balanced, we acquire more facility in using all the possible options for perception (S and N) and for judgment (T and F), for decisiveness (J) and flexibility (P), for extraversion (E) and introversion (I). Jung suggests that the ideal situation for a mature, whole person is that all four of the functions be situated at a midpoint between the conscious and the unconscious parts of our nature.[12] Thus, all of them will be available for use in our conscious activities. In *The Kingdom Within*,[13] John Sanford suggests that this was the situation of Jesus Christ, a fully mature person who was in command of all his faculties for perceiving, judging, and relating.

Different ages of history seem to have their peculiar worldview and temperament. It appears that the present generation is pulled between the Franciscan (SP, which is often considered "free-spirited in the manner of St. Francis of Assisi), and what is often thought of as the more conservative Ignatian (SJ) temperament. This idea is somewhat corroborated by the fact that the majority of those taking part in our Prayer Project during 1982 indicated that the Franciscan type of prayer was their favorite prayer form even though less than 10 percent of them tested as belonging to the SP temperament. The popularity of the Thomistic type of prayer during the previous centuries, as contrasted with that of the Franciscan, Ignatian, and Augustinian prayer styles today, can be explained by the prevailing worldview or temperament of the times having changed.

Bad experiences with a type of prayer which is unsuited to one's temperament will also build up a bias against that type of prayer. Often this prejudice is toward a distorted version of the prayer-form. Whenever one particular method of prayer is recommended as the one and only type of prayer for everyone, a negative attitude toward that kind of prayer soon arises. There is no one form of prayer that is best for every one and for every given occasion. Fanaticism with its harmful divisiveness results when we favor one method of prayer excessively and deny value to the other forms of prayer. To the adherents of one method this acceptance seems at first to bring a certain peace of mind since it does away with the tension required to maintain a balance between opposites. However, denying the value of other forms of prayer deprives us of the spiritual riches available to us when we use all four functions and all four attitudes. This, then, is why we recommend the use of all the different methods of prayer which the Christian tradition has developed during the past twenty-one centuries.

CHAPTER TWO

HOW TEMPERAMENT AFFECTS
CHRISTIAN SPIRITUALITY

While it is not possible to say with certainty what the Myers-Briggs type of any particular historical figure may have been, what we do know about their personalities, actions, attitudes and ways of being in the world allows for reasonable speculation in this regard. With this caveat in mind, consideration of the apparent temperament of each of the original disciples can give us many valuable insights into the way that people of New Testament times, and later generations of Christians, acted and prayed. It does seem clear that the temperament of each of the original disciples and of their successors influenced the direction they took in their relationship with God and in the teachings they passed on to us. What then were the likely dominant attitudes, functions, and temperaments of Jesus, the original apostles, evangelists, and saints who have greatly influence the history of Christianity?

In *The Kingdom Within*,[1] John Sanford points out how Jesus, our Divine Lord, had the ability to use all four functions and all four attitudes in the circumstances of his life. As a fully mature person, Jesus was both Extravert and Introvert, both Sensing and Intuitive, both Thinking and Feeling, both Judging and Perceiving, depending upon the situation. The theory of temperament posits that all of us have some ability in all eight of these areas but that we tend to favor one or the other side of all four sets of preferences. More often than not, we tend to favor our Dominant or Auxiliary Function rather than the opposite which is our Tertiary or Inferior function. The more mature and Christ-like we become, the more balanced we become in the use of all four attitudes and all four functions.

In the providence of God, the four men (Paul, James, John, and Peter) who were most responsible for the spirituality and growth of Christianity in the first century were very likely of the four basic temperaments. St. Paul would be considered of the NF (Intuitive-Feeling) temperament and was continually peeking around the corner to envision new insights about the kingdom of God. It was through St. Paul that Christianity shed most of the oppressive shackles of Mosaic Law, for instance, the law of circumcision.

St. James, whose influence on first century Christianity rivaled that of St. Paul, would seem to have had an SJ (Sensing-Judging) temperament and constantly exhorted the Christians to the duty of implementing their faith into action in every part of their lives. St. James was the conservative who insisted that Christianity keep at least some of the basic Mosaic laws and regulations. (See Acts of the Apostles, Chapter 15:13–21.)

St. John, the beloved disciple and the founder of the Johannine community, was probably an NT (Intuitive-Thinking) temperament. He gave a fresh synthesis of existing ideas which formed Christian theology during the first century. St. John, as a contemplative, was the forerunner of the mystical tradition which, in every age, has been a part of the heritage of Christianity.

Saint Peter, the SP (Sensing-Perceiving) temperament, a man of action, had the responsibility for maintaining peace among the opposing theological schools. We see Peter using his troubleshooting abilities during the Council of Jerusalem to reconcile Paul and James and their followers.

From the point of view of the four functions, James was likely a sensing type; Paul an intuitive type; John, a thinking type; and Peter, a feeling type. Peter and Paul can be seen as extroverts, while John and James were probably introverts. Peter and Paul seem to have been Perceivers (P-type persons), while John and James were likely judgers (J-type persons). Therefore, the type of these four important leaders of the first century Christianity would probably be: Peter – ESFP; Paul – ENFP; John – INTJ; James – ISTJ.

Similarly, due to their individual temperaments, the evangelists (Matthew, Mark, Luke, John) give us four different viewpoints of the character, life events, and teachings of Jesus. St. Matthew was probably an SJ temperament, St. Mark, an SP, Saint Luke, an NF, and St. John, an NT. Each of them looked at the public ministry of Jesus through the eyes of their own temperament, thus giving us four different insights into the richness of the personality and teachings of Jesus. Thus, St. Matthew (SJ) emphasizes continuity with the past by pointing out again and again how Jesus is the fulfillment of the prophecies of the Old Testament. Mark (SP) is very action-oriented, giving only a minimum of the teachings of Jesus.

Luke (NF), on the other hand, is more person-oriented and shows Jesus's great compassion for sinners, women, and outcasts. John (NT) puts great emphasis on the importance of truth and knowledge, and is the most mystical and contemplative of the four evangelists.

Just as to confine our prayer experiences to our dominant and auxiliary functions or temperament would be a mistake, so too it would be a mistake to use exclusively only one Gospel in order to understand the totality of Jesus Christ and his message. Naturally, we will have our favorite Gospel, which is usually the one most closely in accord with our innate temperament; but we will miss some of the deepest experiences of the reality of God if we neglect those Gospels which we find difficult and somewhat contrary to our disposition. While it may be comparatively easy to speculate about the basic temperament (NF, NT, SP, SJ) of the writers of the four Gospels, it is more difficult to determine which of the 16 types they belong to, since we know little about their personality, other than what we can glean from the Gospels they wrote. Nevertheless, to hazard a guess, Matthew very well could have been an ESTJ, Mark an ESFP, Luke, an INFP, and John, an INTJ.

Trinitarian Spirituality and Marian Devotion

During the first three centuries of Christianity the primary concern of spirituality and prayer was the development of the right attitude and relationship with the triune God and especially with Jesus Christ.[2] Along with Trinitarianism, there sprang up a strong Marian devotion which emphasized the feminine and receptive side of prayer and spirituality. By the late third century, prayer to Mary was an important part of the Christian tradition. The earliest known prayer to Mary, the *Sub Tuum Praesidium*.[3] "We fly to thy patronage, O holy Mother of God," goes back to this time. With a little imagination one can easily see how human temperaments and function types helped to solidify both Trinitarian spirituality and Marian devotion. The SJ temperament would be attracted especially to the Heavenly Father with His infinite goodness. The NT temperament would be attracted to Jesus Christ, the Logos, the Word of God, who is Eternal Truth. The NF temperament would be attracted to the Holy Spirit who by love invisibly unites the Church with God the Father and Jesus Christ the Risen Lord. The SP temperament would be attracted to the beauties of Mary with her humility and openness to God. Trinitarian spirituality reached its zenith in the decisions of the Council of Nicaea (325) and the Council of Chalcedon (451). Marian devotion reached a high-water mark with the decisions of the Council of Ephesus (432) when Mary was officially defined *"Theotokos"* or Mother of God.

Looking at Trinitarian and Marian spirituality from the point of view of the four functions, devotion to God the Father highlights the Feeling Function with special emphasis upon God's goodness and mercy. Jesus Christ came on earth to proclaim this good news (Gospel) of God's loving and merciful goodness and to update the Old Testament concept of God from Lord and Creator to that of merciful Father and Provider. God the Son as the divine Logos (Word of God) speaks to the Thinking Function with the new truths and insights which Jesus's Incarnation brought to mankind. God the Holy Spirit manifested in the seven-fold gifts, especially the Gift of Wisdom, calls forth the Intuitive Function, the creativeness of which sees unity not only between Father and Son but also between God and the whole of creation. Finally, devotion to Mary elicits the Sensing Function which is used to appreciate the beauty and order of God's creation. Thus, the four transcendental values of goodness, truth, unity, and beauty represent the spiritual expression of the four functions of Feeling, Thinking, Intuition, and Sensing and are in turn vitalized by devotion to the three persons of the Trinity and the Blessed Mother.

The Spirituality of the Desert Fathers and Mothers

The union of the Church and State under Constantine saw the beginnings of a new spirituality. Bloody martyrdom, or simply the constant possibility of it during the first three centuries, demanded heroic practice of the Gospel teachings. After 313 A.D., when the practice of Christianity was no longer illegal, the mass of Christians began to lead a life of adaptation to the secular world. Because of this "watering down" of the ideal Christian life, many men and women fled to the desert in order to practice asceticism, detachment, and austerity in a cenobitic life in the caves and deserts of Egypt, Palestine, and Syria. This exodus to the desert, begun in the fourth century, resulted in a new type of spirituality known as the "white" martyrdom to distinguish it from the "red" or bloody martyrdom of the previous centuries. St. Jerome and John Cassian are two well-known devout men from the West who went to the Desert Fathers to study and to learn this new desert spirituality.

When we study the spirituality of the desert fathers and mothers, we find that they made full use of the four psychological functions during prayer. Sensing: they practiced mortification of their senses in order to open their souls to the Spirit. Thinking: there was daily meditation upon the basic truths of faith as revealed in the Scriptures. Feeling: they attempted to maintain a constant, personal relationship with God the Father, Jesus the Risen Lord, and the Holy Spirit. Intuition: they experienced a deep, contemplative union with God. In desert spirituality, all four basic temperaments were brought into operation. The SJ (Ignatian) temperament occupied itself with daily Gospel meditation. The SP (Franciscan) temperament spent the waking period of the day and frequently much of the night in spontaneous prayer. The NF (Augustinian) temperament was constantly striving to attain and maintain a deep, personal relationship with God and Jesus; while the NT (Thomistic) temperament emphasized a deep, contemplative, mystical union with God. This appeal to all the functions and temperaments is the reason for the popularity of desert spirituality and prayer over the centuries.

Two types of prayer were developed in the West from the wisdom and experience of the Desert Fathers and Mothers. John Cassian introduced to the convents of monks and nuns in the monastic communities of the West the continual meditation or rumination on Scripture, which became the well-known *Lectio Divina* of the Rule of St. Benedict. Cassian also learned from Abba Isaac, and the other monks in the deserts of Egypt, another form of meditation which today is popularly called "centering prayer."[4] This same form of prayer became popular in Greece and Russia where it was called the "Jesus Prayer."[5] The Jesus Prayer and centering prayer activate all four psychological functions to establish a mystical union between God and oneself.[6] The senses (Sensing) are used in the constant repetition of the words, "Lord Jesus Christ, have mercy on me, a sinner." This constant repetition, accompanied by meditation on Jesus as Savior (Thinking Function), results in an ever deeper personal relationship with Jesus (Feeling Function). Finally, the constant repetition of these words hundreds of times each day can activate the Intuitive Function and result in mystical contemplation.

Benedictine Spirituality

First introduced into the West by John Cassian and later developed and used by St. Benedict in the rule of his monastic communities, *Lectio Divina* has, over the centuries, been closely identified with Benedictine prayer and spirituality. This ancient type of prayer has probably been used by Christians more often than any other method of prayer. This is understandable since it employs all four psychological functions and therefore is an ideal form of prayer for all the different types and temperaments of personality. Four other traditional forms of Christian spirituality and prayer – Augustinian, Franciscan, Thomistic, and Ignatian – are actually variations of this most ancient of all Christian forms of prayer. The *Devotio Moderna* of the late Middle Ages also includes all four steps of *Lectio Divina*. In Chapter Three, we explain more fully the four steps of *Lectio Divina* and how they make use of all four functions of Sensing, Thinking, Feeling, and Intuition. We will also suggest some examples of how one might use *Lectio Divina* in a daily period of prayer.

Augustinian Spirituality

Throughout the Christian era, the Church Fathers and spiritual masters have taught that the words of the Bible can be transposed to relate to the needs of every individual and every generation. The inspired writers of the Bible were able to penetrate the eternal wisdom of God and applied their insights to the situations of their time; yet the infinite wisdom of God is applicable to all times and all situations of mankind. Without exception, the Fathers and Doctors of the Church have practiced transposition of the Words of God as part of their daily prayer and taught their disciples to use this same method to discern the path God willed for them. We call this method Augustinian Prayer. St. Augustine was not the only one who taught personal reflection on the presence of God in His Word. However, the Rule of St. Augustine,[7] which he developed for the communities established by him, became the basic method of spirituality followed by many religious communities in succeeding centuries. Thus, we honor him by naming this type of prayer Augustinian.

Augustinian prayer uses all four functions but special emphasis is placed upon the use of Intuition and Feeling, making it especially adaptable to the NF temperament. St. Augustine, as well as a great many canonized saints, spiritual masters, and seekers of The Way, are more than likely to be of the NF temperament. Of the four basic temperaments this temperament has the greatest drive for self-development and spiritual growth.[8] In Chapter Five, we will explain more fully the Augustinian method of prayer and give some examples for your use.

Franciscan Spirituality

At the beginning of the thirteenth century, St. Francis of Assisi revolutionized the Church and the medieval world by introducing a new type of spirituality, which attracted not only large numbers of the ordinary lay people but also clergy and religious, and won the approval of the Popes and the Roman Curia. St. Francis probably understood the Gospel teaching of Jesus as well as, or better than, any Christian of any age. Once he was converted to the Lord, he resolved to follow the Gospel as literally and totally as possible. The result was a way of prayer and spirituality totally open to the guidance of the Holy Spirit and with a simplicity and directness that could be understood easily even by the uneducated.

Many have followed Franciscan spirituality and prayer in every century, and it seems to have a special appeal today.[9] In the responses to our prayer questionnaires during the Prayer Project, there was a strong preference for the Franciscan type of prayer by all personality types. This is understandable since we are living in a period that has a free-spirited and open attitude. Many of us today are Franciscans at heart and are charmed with the spirit of abandon, humor, and magnetism revealed in the human-interest anecdotes we have heard and read about St. Francis. However, there is more to Franciscan spirituality than the poetry of a free spirit who rejoices in the beauties and glories of God in nature.

St. Francis is called *il poverello,* the poor little man, because he made a deliberate decision to give away all his worldly possessions and depend solely upon the charity of others for everything, even the bread he ate. How many of us are willing to adopt this aspect of Franciscan spirituality? With all of our concern about security, insurance, savings and investments, etc., can we honestly say that we are willing to undertake the Franciscan way of blind, total trust in God? We are probably so far removed from the poverty of St. Francis that for us even to imagine how it might be put into practice today is nearly impossible. The modern attraction to St. Francis is one more way that divine grace is calling us to divest ourselves of our excessive attachment to worldly goods and material prosperity and follow the way of *il poverello*.

St. Ignatius of Loyola states that the third and highest degree of humility is the desire to be like Jesus Christ to the extent of desiring to suffer the same afflictions, the same rejection and persecution, the same hatred and torture as Jesus did. St. Francis so desired union with the sufferings of Jesus that before he died he experienced the Stigmata, the same wounds that Jesus suffered on the cross. These open wounds shed blood and severely pained Francis during the last years of his life. An additional humiliation occurred when the brothers of his own community turned against him and rejected him as their leader in favor of Brother Elias. This third and highest degree of humility is beautifully illustrated in the story of how St. Francis taught Brother Leo that perfect joy is to be found not in heroic deeds but in bearing the Cross.[10]

The basic temperament of St. Francis was SP (Sensing Perceiving); and we have called the type of prayer and spirituality which especially appeals to the SP temperament Franciscan prayer and spirituality. In Chapter Six, we will explain this type of prayer and give some Franciscan prayer exercises for one to use.

Thomistic Spirituality

At the same time that Francis of Assisi was developing his spirituality in Italy, another type of spirituality was being developed in Spain and France by St. Dominic. Dominican spirituality developed in the large medieval universities of Paris, Bologna, and elsewhere, and had special appeal to the intellectuals of the day in their search of truth. The most famous son of St. Dominic was St. Thomas Aquinas who lived a generation after St. Dominic's death. Because of the tremendous influence of the theology of St. Thomas on the spirituality of so many Christians, instead of calling this spirituality and prayer Dominican, we call it Thomistic.

Thomistic prayer appeals especially to the NT temperament with its interest and search for truth and competency. It has been popular among the intellectual leaders of Roman Catholicism and also among Protestant leaders of the Enlightenment down through the centuries until the present era. However, unless they happened to be of the NT temperament, most individuals found this type of prayer especially difficult. Yet, this method was most often recommended in the books on prayer during the Enlightenment and throughout the Tridentine Period of Catholicity, right up to the Second Vatican Council. Because the impression was given that this type of prayer was the *best* method of prayer and should be used by all, many – including priests and the religious trained in seminaries and monasteries – found prayer difficult or dry and often abandoned its practice. In Chapter Seven, we explain Thomistic prayer more fully and give some practical ways to use it.

Devotio Moderna

During the fourteenth and fifteenth centuries there was a reaction against the over-emphasis by the Scholastics on intellectuality and excessive use of the Thinking Function. In the low countries of Holland and Belgium a new form of prayer – *Devotio Moderna* – developed. The great emphasis was upon the use of the Feeling Function in prayer. Gerard Groote and Thomas à Kempis are the two best known advocates of this new form of prayer and spirituality. From this period comes the book, *The Imitation of Christ*, which was popularly attributed to Thomas à Kempis. These words taken from *The Imitation of Christ:* "I would rather feel contrition than know how to define it,"[11] clearly express the anti-intellectual attitude of this spirituality.

Emphasis on feeling in prayer has continued and is evidenced in the French spirituality of the eighteenth and nineteenth centuries. St. Thérèse of Lisieux is a modern example of the *Devotio Moderna* spirituality. Even as a young teenager, St. Thérèse had memorized *The Imitation of Christ* in its entirety and could quote it chapter by chapter. The modern version of the *Devotio Moderna* was somewhat sugary and distasteful to many; but in recent years, people are once more appreciating its value and depth.

Ignatian Spirituality

Following the pattern of the thirteenth century when two well known forms of spirituality developed under the guidance of St. Francis and St. Dominic, in the sixteenth century two well-known Spanish saints developed two types of spirituality. One of them was St. Ignatius of Loyola, founder of the Jesuit Order.

Shortly after his conversion, St. Ignatius went alone into a cave at Manresa and in the course of 30 days had an experience of prayer that profoundly influenced the rest of his life. He later developed this type of prayer into what is known as *The Spiritual Exercises of St. Ignatius.*[12] The meditational process of the *Exercises* is more easily understood by the SJ temperament, but the NT and NF temperament also find this method of praying quite profitable. However, the SP temperament frequently has difficulty with this method of prayer. Most souls who are willing to endure the discipline of the 30 days of intense prayer activity of *The Ignatian Spiritual Exercises* are rewarded with an unforgettable spiritual experience that frequently changes the whole direction of their life. Somewhat resembling Augustinian prayer, Ignatian Prayer differs in that it *projects the* person as a participant into the different scenes and experiences of the life of Jesus and history of salvation; whereas Augustinian Prayer *transposes* the words of the Bible to our situation today. The spirituality of the liturgical[13] year where we commemorate the events of salvation history, especially the events in the life of Jesus, is a good example of Ignatian spirituality. This type of prayer is explained more fully in Chapter Four and suggestions for its use are given.

Teresian Spirituality

The other well-known sixteenth century Spanish saint is the Carmelite nun Teresa of Avila. St. Teresa treats many different forms of prayer in her writings, but she is most famous for her discussion of prayer for those who have reached the higher levels of passive contemplation. In the terminology of St. Teresa these would be the types of prayer appropriate to those who have reached the fourth, fifth, sixth, and seventh spiritual mansions.[14] Just as the Benedictine *Lectio Divina* is appropriate for all types and temperaments, so are St. Teresa's recommendations for contemplation suitable for all types of human personality. St. John of the Cross with his discussion of the "dark nights," which are frequently endured by contemplatives, gives another dimension of Teresian prayer and spirituality. In this book we do not give a full explanation of Teresian contemplation since it does not seem to depend upon temperament but stands in a class by itself and is practiced by all temperaments and personalities.[15]

CHAPTER THREE

BENEDICTINE PRAYER:
LECTIO DIVINA

Lectio Divina is a type of prayer suitable to all four basic temperaments: SJ, SP, NF, and NT. It also employs to full advantage all of the four psychological functions: Sensing, Intuition, Thinking, and Feeling. Both Judging Types and Perceiving Types like this method since it can be either as structured or as flexible as one chooses. Furthermore, *Lectio Divina* can be used by Extraverts in relating to the outer world or by Introverts in relating to the inner world of the spirit. Therefore, it is no surprise that it is both one of the oldest and most popular of all forms of prayer in the Christian tradition.

Lectio Divina is a method of prayer that goes back to the fourth and fifth centuries. Easily and quickly translated as "sacred reading," it can be only that. Or, using sacred reading as the base, it becomes a ladder of escalation or intensification of prayer with four steps: reading, meditation, prayer, and contemplation. Traditionally, we use the four Latin equivalents to express these steps: Lectio, Meditatio, Oratio, Contemplatio.

In all likelihood the monastic practice of *Lectio Divina* was brought to the West from the Eastern desert fathers by John Cassian at the beginning of the fifth century. However, it has been closely connected to St. Benedict and Benedictine spirituality since its development and popularity began in the communities of monks and nuns founded by St. Benedict. Furthermore, this method of prayer is highly recommended even today by Benedictines and Cistercians. Many later forms of prayer developed by Christians are based upon this prayer method. As different versions of *Lectio Divina,* they use and emphasize the four psychological functions: Sensing, Intuition, Thinking, and Feeling. Therefore, we find this form of prayer is appropriate for all four of the basic temperaments and all sixteen individual types of human personality.

Corresponding to the four basic psychological functions, there are four steps to *Lectio Divina* which call forth the use of each of these functions. (1) Lectio uses the Senses either in spiritual reading or in perceiving the works of the Lord. (2) Meditatio uses the psychological function of Thinking (the intellect) to reflect upon the insights presented in Lectio. (3) Oratio calls forth one's Feeling Function to personalize the new insights so that one may enter into a personal dialogue or communication with God. (4) Finally, in Contemplatio, one's Intuition is used in order to coalesce the experience of the previous three steps. In this time of quiet, one is open to the inspirations of the Holy Spirit which may come by way of new insights, new perceptions, or a new infusion of peace, joy, and love which the saints tell us is part of the mystical union.

In the twelfth century, the Carthusian Prior Guigo II describes *Lectio Divina* in *The Ladder of Monks* (Section X): "Reading, you should seek; meditating, you will find; praying, you shall call; and contemplating, the door will be opened to you." And there is the contemporary description of *Lectio Divina* by a Southern rural minister who, when asked how he prayed, replied: "I reads myself full; I thinks myself clear; I prays myself hot; I lets myself cool."

The four steps of *Lectio Divina* respond to the characteristics of all four of the basic temperaments. Lectio, or spiritual reading, appeals especially to the SJ temperament within each of us. Through it we study and search the Scriptures and other religious writings to discover within this wisdom of the ages the direction and guidance for our daily life. Meditatio, or reflection, upon these ideas and insights culled from the spiritual reading gives answers to the NT (seeking) temperament. In this portion of *Lectio Divina,* we try to personalize the message received in Lectio either by transposition or projection. In transposition (the Augustinian method), we try to imagine these words being spoken directly to us, i.e., as if God or Jesus is speaking to us personally. In projection (the Ignatian method), we put ourselves back into the biblical situation and try to imagine that we are present as the words or events first occurred and then try to draw some practical fruit from this experience.

The third part of *Lectio Divina,* Oratio, appeals both to the NF and the SP temperaments. In this step we dialogue with the Lord and respond personally to what He has said to us. Thus, we enter into an intimate relationship with God, Jesus, and the Holy Spirit. Feelings of love, joy, gratitude, sorrow, repentance, desire, enthusiasm, conviction, commitment are activated and verbalized in spontaneous prayers of love, thanksgiving, sorrow, dedication, and petition.

The fourth portion, Contemplatio, is a time just to be quiet, to listen, and to be open to whatever the Lord might wish to impart. The creatively perceptive NF temperament sees this fourth step as an introduction to the contemplative type of prayer of which all of us are capable. We can expect some distractions at this time, but they should not disturb us. When one becomes aware of distractions, one simply recalls the theme of the Lectio and tries once again to be open and attentive to whatever new perceptions, insights, inspirations, thoughts, or practical applications that appear. This fourth part might be thought of as "resting in the Lord" – just being present to the enjoyment of being alone with Him. This is a time for the activation of our intuitive faculties in order to catch any reconciling symbols[1] that might emerge from the depths of our unconscious.

Lectio Divina is a method of prayer that is suitable for both the beginner and the spiritually advanced. Its progress from hearing the Word of God to studying it, reflecting upon it, praying upon it, and adapting it to our situation leads one deeper and deeper into the longed-for union with God. By considering each step on this ladder of prayer, we can see how we may be helped on our spiritual journey.

Lectio

Lectio is the eager seeking after the Word of God and divine truth and the way by which God's truth is imparted to us. The revelation of God's truth is found primarily in the Sacred Scriptures; but God also reveals His Presence in other books, in created nature, in other people, in the events of history, and in the events of divine providence. God usually reveals His truth through the works of other human beings who have discovered and shared it through their writings, their lives, their works of art, and other forms of expression. The authors of the books of the Bible were inspired by the Holy Spirit, so we believe the Holy Spirit is the primary author of these books. But God also inspires others and speaks to us through the words and works of all his creatures.

Meditatio

As long as the Word of God is in a book, or in nature, or in the word and work of someone else, it will not have the effect upon us that God intends it to have. Therefore, through Meditatio we must welcome the Word of God into our lives and turn it from a dead word into the living word and presence of God. Having received God's truth, we need to chew it and ruminate upon it as a cow does upon its cud. Through meditation we discover the beauty and goodness of God's truth and apply it to our own situation and needs. Thus, we bring to life the meaning of divine revelation as we personalize and adapt it to our daily living.

Oratio

Our response to this revealed truth is the Oratio. We can accept the Word of God or dismiss its value for us. We are free to reflect and meditate upon it and try to relate its meaning to our life; or we can reject it as of no worth or no value to us. In the Oratio we decide what changes we want to make in our life as a result of the truth of God that has been revealed to us. At this time, we decide whether we will incorporate the Word of God into our hearts, our lives, and our work or whether we will rationalize a rejection of its efficacy for us. Our response is expressed through words, thoughts, desires, feelings, resolutions, decisions, commitments, and dedications; or through sorrow for past failures; through gratitude, praise, and petition.

In this third step of *Lectio Divina,* we use the four different kinds of prayer described in the old Baltimore Catechism: Adoration, Contrition, Thanksgiving, and Supplication. As an aid to perk our memory the acronym, ACTS, was coined. It is important to note that these four types of prayer (adoration, contrition, thanksgiving, and supplication or petition) belong to the third step of *Lectio Divina.* All of them are part of our personal response to God's Word. To limit our prayer merely to these four responses to God's Word would be a grave error. Prayer is a dialogue in which we both listen to God and then respond to Him. All too often we limit prayer to a monologue of our speaking to God, and even limit that primarily to petition or supplication. True prayer is, first and foremost, listening to God speaking to us and then, secondarily, responding to God's words to us.

Contemplatio

In Contemplatio, we seek to affect the union of love that should result from our dialogue with God. This is meant to be the consummation of the union of our mind and God's truth, of our heart and God's love, of our life and God's life, of our person and the person of God. This consummation can be neither hurried nor forced. We need to give ample time and undistracted attention to the word, truth, or task at hand if we hope to experience any kind of mystical union with God here on earth.

Frequently, we will go through the whole exercise of *Lectio Divina* without being aware of this union with God occurring. If so, it is quite possible that through either some fault of our own or circumstances beyond our control (i.e., outside interruptions and distractions) we were not properly disposed for this union with God. On the other hand, this action can be so quiet, so deep, and so spiritual that we are not consciously aware of it happening, but there is a way to know if it has occurred. Our Lord says: "By your fruits you will know them" (Matt 7: 16) and St. Paul tells us the fruits of the Holy Spirit are: "love, joy, peace, patience, generosity, faithfulness, kindness, gentleness, self-control, purity" (Gal 5:22- 23). If we become aware later that there has been an increase in any one of these attributes within us, we can be assured that our *Lectio Divina* has been successful and God has truly touched and reached us.

Aids for the Use of *Lectio Divina*

There are certain things we can do to make the prayer period in which we use *Lectio Divina* more rewarding and uplifting. First, we should choose the time of the day when we are most alert, least distracted, least tired, most well-rested, and without outside pressure. In other words, we should set aside prime time each day for prayer. Secondly, we should seek a place that is quiet and restful, warm or cool as needed, comfortable, and conducive to giving our full attention to God and God's Word.

Having found the best possible time and place for one's prayer, one should select a passage of Sacred Scripture, or some other spiritual reading, appropriate to one's present needs. There are many ways to make a choice of the proper text. One may follow a recommended list of texts or topics from some book or leaflet. One may simply take a whole book of the Bible, like one of the Gospels, and read it through slowly, chapter by chapter, while consulting a good commentary on the text. If possible, this process of hunting and fishing to discover the text, or word, or idea that speaks to us and is appropriate for prayer and reflection should be done beforehand, perhaps the previous night. Then we will be ready to use this text on the following day for our period of *Lectio Divina*.

The next day at the selected time we should read the chosen text again slowly several times, trying to savor each word and phrase, making sure that we come to a good understanding of what the text is saying. It sometimes helps to read the text aloud. Then Meditatio, or reflect, upon the text follows, as we try to personalize it so that it speaks to our particular needs. It is helpful to have a notebook or pad of paper handy to note insights and reflections. Our notes should be read over several times and reflected upon, and new insights should be added as they occur. From time to time, we should go back to the text originally selected and reread it to discover if some innuendo or insight was missed. Then record this finding in the notebook and again reread the material in the notebook.

The third step, Oratio, is our response to the Word of God. This can easily be intermingled with the Meditatio so that together these two become a dialogue between God and ourselves. God speaks to us; and we respond with gratitude, love, petition, contrition, praise, sorrow, joy, commitment, dedication. Listening and responding to God can go on for a long time; and the dialogue can become intensely personal, intimate, and full of emotion. A heartfelt reaction of some kind should occur if the prayer is to have lasting results and bring about a change in our life. The feelings may be deep but without visible manifestation, such as tears; but we should be seriously committed to whatever we say to God in response to His Word. Of course, there will be days when we are so tired or distracted that our feelings are not aroused; but, if we have the right intention and make the effort, God will be satisfied; and the time spent will not be wasted.

In the final step, Contemplatio, we must give God ample opportunity to reveal Himself anew to us. God must never be hurried. He sets the pace and keeps His own time schedule. Therefore, we must be willing to wait upon the Lord. We do not tell Him what, or when, or how, but let Him tell us. This requires silence, stillness, and a willingness to wait until the Lord Himself moves our heart, stirs up our will, and enlightens our mind. "Be still and know that I am God" (Psalm 46: 11). Having prepared ourselves by reading, meditation, and prayer, we now await and hope for whatever graces God might see fit to send our way. Many times, we will not be aware of anything happening, but we should trust that the grace of God is working within the depths of our soul. God asks blind faith and trust of us.

The four steps of Lectio Divina may be followed in any order we choose so that one may go from one to the other and then back again. For example, quiet periods for contemplation can be interspersed throughout the reading, meditation, and oration. Meditation and oration can be used interchangeably, going from one to the other and then back again. Also, one should return frequently to rereading the text in order to discern any new insights. Complete freedom should be followed in the order and variety of the four steps during the prayer period. One must try to be completely open to the guidance and inspirations of the Holy Spirit. This means going with our thoughts in whatever direction that seems right and best at the time. We should never hesitate to experiment and try new ways so that we may discover the method best suited to our needs at the time.

A spiritual journal is frequently a great help to people when using *Lectio Divina*. This journal may be an ordinary notebook in which we write all or part of any exchanges between God and ourselves that occur during the time set aside for prayer. In it we note any insights that come to us during our reading, meditation, and contemplation. We also enter in it our responses during the Oratio or other times during the prayer period. Such a written record of our dialogue with God is a wonderful way of imprinting our prayer experiences upon our memory so that we can more easily recall them later when needed.

15 *Lectio Divina* Prayer Suggestions

These suggestions are based upon the Sunday selections from St. Matthew's Gospel, Cycle A, 10th to 24th Sundays of Ordinary Time. It is suggested that at least one commentary be used in connection with the prayer period. The commentary referred to is *Matthew* by John P. Meier.[2]

~ Prayer Suggestion 1 ~

Lectio

Read Matthew 9:9–13 and Meier, pp. 92–95.

Meditatio

Jesus came to call sinners, the unworthy. God is merciful. Therefore, none of us need ever be discouraged or imagine that we are unworthy of being in the presence of God and Christ. However, having received God's gracious invitation and assurance of mercy and forgiveness, we now have the duty to follow Jesus in his example of mercy and forgiveness toward those who have offended us. This also means following Jesus in a life of victimhood, The Way of The Cross.

Oratio

Respond to the call of Jesus by inviting him to join in a fellowship conversation. Dialogue with him, tell him our joy at his Good News and our gratitude for God's mercy and forgiveness. Resolve to be ready to forgive others and to be united with those who have offended us. This is the time to make known to ourselves and to the Lord our resolutions of how we intend to follow Jesus in The Way of the Cross and victimhood.

Contemplatio

Be still and be open to any insights, thoughts, desires, resolutions, peace, joy, or love that come to our attention.

~ Prayer Suggestion 2 ~

Lectio

Read Matthew 9:36 to 10:8 and Meier, pp. 100–107.

Meditatio

The compassion of Jesus for the people of his time is the model for our own compassion for the people of our time who are wandering aimlessly, not knowing where to go. Not only should we pray for vocations to Christian ministry, but we ourselves should also respond to the call to ministry. Having been summoned to ministry by Jesus, we are given the power and authority to expel unclean spirits, cure sickness and disease, which would include spiritual diseases. All of this should be done freely without asking anything in return except what is necessary to sustain one's life and ministry. "Freely you have received, freely you should give."

Oratio

Respond personally to the call of Jesus to ministry. Pray not only for the call of others but that you too will respond generously to God's call.

Contemplatio

Be open to any thought, desires, insights concerning how one might do more in ministering to others.

~ Prayer Suggestion 3 ~

Lectio

Read Matthew 10:26–33 and Meier, pp. 111–112.

Meditatio

What are my present fears in regard to my ministry? What is it, or who is it, that presently intimidates me? Where have I failed to minister because of fear? What does this Gospel passage say in regard to overcoming these fears? The only one we need to fear is God, yet Jesus assures us that we are worth more to God than all of the created world. The only time we need to fear is when we are ashamed of our relationship to Christ and disown it before the people of this world. Where and when have I hidden my Christianity and remained silent?

Oratio

Beg God for the courage to profess one's faith regardless of the situation or person and ask His forgiveness for this fear which shows a lack of faith.

Contemplatio

Maintain silence in order to catch any new insights.

~ Prayer Suggestion 4 ~

Lectio

Read Matthew 10:37–42 and Meier, pp. 112–115.

Meditatio

Where have I sought only myself in my work, in my family, in my recreation, in my leisure time, in my church work? Can I think of some instances in my life where the seeking of self has brought ruin upon whatever I was doing? Can I think of an instance where I have sacrificed myself for the sake of God or others? What happened as a result?

Oratio

Pray for the grace to put oneself last and God and others first.

Contemplatio

Be open to any insights about the value of self-sacrifice.

~ Prayer Suggestion 5 ~

Lectio

Read Matthew 11:25–30 and Meier, pp. 126–128.

Meditatio

Jesus gives us an example from his own life of how we should pray. How much is this like our own way of praying? Do gratitude and praise of God predominate our thoughts? Do we show the same gracious acceptance of God's will in our regard? What can we change in our present life to allow Jesus to reveal himself and the Father to us?

How do we respond to the gentle, loving invitation

of Jesus to come to him when we are heavily laden? Jesus says, "Learn from me for I am gentle, meek, humble, and lowly of heart." What would this involve in our life? What changes would be needed? Jesus assures us that his yoke is easy and his burden light. Have we found this to be true? What does carrying the yoke of service for Christ involve?

Oratio

There is much food for personal response to Jesus in this passage. Try to activate feelings of love, joy, generosity, contrition, dedication. Try to pray to the Heavenly Father in the same way that Jesus does in this passage.

Contemplatio

Read these words of Jesus over several times and then just be quiet and allow their meaning to sink deeply into your mind, conscience, heart, and soul.

~ Prayer Suggestion 6 ~

Lectio

Read Matthew 13:1–23 and Meier, pp. 141–146.

Meditatio

Jesus gives six different results of his sowing of the seed. Three of them do not produce any fruit, but three of them do: 30-, 60-, and 100-fold. Think of the different times in your life where these six situations have occurred. There have been times when we have heard the Word of God, say at Sunday liturgy, but before we get home, we have totally forgotten it (the first situation!). There have been times when we have heard the Word with great enthusiasm; but a week later it has withered away (second group!). Think of the times when we have heard God's word, applied it to our situation, and have done something in response to it for a while, but then the cares and concerns of this world have choked out our good resolution s so that no good fruit resulted. Think also of the times when God's Word did produce good and abundant fruit in our life – perhaps even a hundred-fold.

Oratio

Having applied the parable to our own life, respond accordingly. There probably will be room for contrition, regret for past failures, fervent prayers for help in the present, good resolutions for the future. What can you say to God to ensure that you will be in one of the groups who produce good fruit rather than in one of those who fail to produce any fruit?

Contemplatio

What new insights is the Holy Spirit giving you from reflecting on this parable of the sower and the seed?

~ Prayer Suggestion 7 ~

Lectio

Read Matthew 13:24–43 and Meier, pp. 147–151.

Meditatio

This parable of the cockle and the wheat can be applied either to our need of tolerance and patience with others in our community who seem to represent the cockle or to the mixture of good and bad in our own life. Where have we been too energetic in our attempts to root up the cockle in our community before the time of harvest? How should we show more patience with our own faults, the weeds or cockle within our character? The dividing line between good and evil (wheat and cockle) runs through the middle of our heart as well as through the middle of the hearts of other individuals and communities. There is a right time to root out the faults that have been allowed to grow up beside the virtues. It would be harmful if we tried to eradicate them too quickly. What then are the particular faults that at present we should be trying to root up and remove from our soul.

Oratio

We should pray fervently for light and guidance from the Holy Spirit to discern the cockle (faults) in our life. Pray also that the little mustard seed, or leaven of God's grace, will not be allowed to die out or be

47

wasted. With patience we can hope that it will grow until our whole life is shot through with God.

Contemplatio

Be perfectly quiet and try to discern God's time schedule in regard to conquering the various faults of our personality. At what does the Lord wish us to work at this time?

~ Prayer Suggestion 8 ~

Lectio

Read Matthew 13:44–52 and Meier, pp. 151–154.

Meditatio

What is the hidden treasure and the pearl of great price which is awaiting our discovery? "The reign of God (or the kingdom of God) is like a hidden treasure or pearl of great price." Have we discovered the reign (the kingdom) of God in our life? What does this mean? It is that situation where God and God's will become the center of our whole life, our every thought, word, deed, decision, desire. Once we have discovered this, we should be ready to sacrifice everything to obtain it. Is this true in my life? The kingdom of God is the situation where God has total freedom to do whatever he pleases with us and with the world. We are able to use our freedom to thwart God's will for us and thus hinder or hold back the establishment of the kingdom of God.

Oratio

With as much feeling as possible, beg God for the grace to discover, recognize, and appreciate the value of the kingdom of God in one's life. Having discovered its meaning, one can devote one's whole energy to attaining it and pay whatever the price needed to obtain it. Beg God for the grace to sacrifice everything else if necessary.

Contemplatio

Be open to uncovering the particular meaning of the kingdom of God for you in your life. Be open to the price to be paid in order to obtain it.

~ Prayer Suggestion 9 ~

Lectio

Read Matthew 14:13–21 and Meier, pp. 161–163.

Meditatio

Jesus has compassion on the multitude. Today, a multitude of the world's people are hungry and dying of famine. What can we do to relieve this poverty and destitution? God continues to perform on earth the multiplication of the loaves and fishes; for there is more than enough land and opportunity to feed all. The problem is one of distribution. Just as in the Gospel story Jesus depended upon his disciples to distribute the loaves and fishes, we too, his disciples, have a responsibility to bring about a more equitable distribution of the riches of the world today. What am I doing about this? What can I do?

Oratio

Pray for the grace and courage to do something about the world's hunger.

Contemplatio

Be open to any inspirations that God may wish to give.

~ Prayer Suggestion 10 ~

Lectio

Read Matthew 14:22–33 and Meier, pp. 163–166.

Meditatio

Jesus comes walking on the water to save us whenever we are in trouble and when the winds of adversity are against us. His appearance startles us at times, but he reassures us, "Get hold of yourselves. It is I, do not be afraid." Once Jesus joins us in our boat, the winds of adversity quickly die down. We, too, can walk on water. Think of the different times we have had an experience similar to that of Peter.

Oratio

When have we failed to recognize Jesus's approach when we were in danger? Where have we acted like Peter and faltered in our faith? What can we do to assure our recognition of Him in time of trouble? How can we build up our courage and trust?

Contemplatio

Be still and accept a deeper faith and trust in God.

~ Prayer Suggestion 11 ~

Lectio

Read Matthew 15:21–28 and Meier, pp. 171–173.

Meditatio

Jesus finds it impossible to resist the faith and persistence of the Canaanite woman. If we are persistent in our petitions and ask with faith, we too will be irresistible when we pray to the Lord. Where are we lacking in our faith when we go to God in prayer? What within us needs healing at present? What demon that oppresses us do we need to ask the Lord to remove?

Oratio

During this part of our prayer period, let us try to follow the example of the woman in the Gospel when we make our requests. Make sure that what we ask for is in accord with God's will; otherwise always ask on the condition that it be in accord with His will. "Not my will, but your will, O God, be done." Show the same humility as this woman and reflect upon our own lowliness; but like her, do not take "no" for an answer. Be persistent but humble in petitioning.

Contemplatio

Be open to any changes in our way of praying that God might be asking.

~ Prayer Suggestion 12 ~

Lectio

Read Matthew 16:13–20 and Meier, pp. 178–183.

Meditatio

"Who do you say that I am?" What does Jesus mean to me? How often do I think of him in the course of an ordinary day? Is he truly the center of my life? What more can I do to make him the center of my every thought, desire, word, deed? In what way can we say that the church community in which we live is also built upon the rock of our faith? What can I do to increase my faith in Jesus Christ?

Oratio

Pray to Jesus for the faith of Peter. Pray that all whose faith is dependent upon you will be strengthened in their faith in Jesus Christ and their faith not be weakened or lost because of something you may do or fail to do.

Contemplatio

Seek any new insights that might come concerning Jesus Christ.

~ Prayer Suggestion 13 ~

Lectio

Read Matthew 16:21–27 and Meier, pp. 183–188.

Meditatio

What does "to deny myself and take up my cross and follow in the footsteps of Jesus" mean in my life? What are the crosses in my present life? How in today's world can I be a victim of love after the example of Jesus? How is God asking me to lose my life for His sake? Do I deserve the same rebuke as Peter for my attitude toward suffering and sacrifice? How do I make the same mistake as Peter in judging by the standards of this world rather than by the standards of God?

Oratio

Try to put yourself in the place of Peter and imagine how he must have felt to be so severely rebuked by Jesus. Enter with as much feeling as possible into Jesus's struggle to accept the cross that the Heavenly Father willed for him to carry. Be open to the full trauma of Jesus's teaching about the necessity to deny ourselves and take up our cross and follow him on the road to Calvary. Pray for the grace to accept whatever crosses God's providence sees fit to allow to come into our life.

Contemplatio

Be open to the insights about suffering and self-denial which the Lord may impart at this time.

~ Prayer Suggestion 14 ~

Lectio

Read Matthew 18:15-20 and Meier, pp. 204-206.

Meditatio

In this passage, Jesus teaches us one of the most difficult of all the works of mercy: admonishing the sinner. Very few people are able to do a good job of this act of charity, namely, helping others to recognize their faults and do something about changing their lives. Think of the times in one's own life where one has criticized another for some fault but did more harm than good. Can you think of some time when fraternal correction was successful? What can you do to be more successful in carrying out this particular work of mercy? Is there anyone you should attempt to admonish – for example, someone who drinks too much or indulges in some other excess? Jesus says we should first attempt the fraternal correction alone; and then, if necessary, take another when we attempt the intervention; finally, if the situation is serious enough, bring it to the attention of the whole community.

Oratio

Having considered a situation where one might practice fraternal correction, pray fervently for the light to know how best to handle it and for the courage to do it.

Contemplatio

Be open to the guidance of the Holy Spirit.

~ Prayer Suggestion 15 ~

Lectio

Read Matthew 18:21–35 and Meier, pp. 207–209.

Meditatio

Jesus says that we must be willing to forgive seventy-times-seven. This can apply to the something which may have occurred many years ago but caused such a deep hurt that even though we have previously forgiven the person we need to reinstitute the process of forgiveness again and again. Unless we willingly forgive our neighbor, God will not forgive us our faults. Is there anyone who has hurt me in the past that I have not yet forgiven completely? What do I do about it now?

Oratio

Pray the Lord's Prayer, especially the second part, and try to mean it as deeply and sincerely as possible. Pray for each person who has in some way hurt or offended you in the past. This is the first step to forgiveness.

Contemplatio

Be open to the possibility that one needs to forgive again and again.

CHAPTER FOUR

IGNATIAN PRAYER
& SPIRITUALITY:
THE SJ TEMPERAMENT

The method of prayer which we call Ignatian Prayer is a way of prayer even more ancient than the Lectio Divina which was developed in the fourth century. This way of praying was used by the Israelites a thousand to twelve hundred years before the birth of Christ. Its basic trait is the remembrance of an event of salvation history. This commemoration, however, is more than a pious recalling of an event which occurred many years previously; for by immersion in its recollection the praying people relive, participate in, and in a symbolic way make real the past events. All four functions are involved and the same structure is followed as in Lectio Divina. Among Christians, St. Ignatius of Loyola, the founder of the Jesuit Order, was the great teacher of this way of praying. Hence, we have called this type of prayer and spirituality Ignatian in his honor.

The Spiritual Exercises, which were written by Ignatius after an intense spiritual experience in a cave in Manresa where he had retired to pray, give us an outline to follow and commemorate the life of our Lord Jesus Christ. Those employing the Ignatian method of prayer strive to participate in the actual event by projecting themselves back into the historical happening to try to become a part of the scene in order to draw some practical fruit for their life. The sensible imagination[1] is employed so that by reliving the event in an effective manner one can come to real sorrow, joy, or resolution of amendment. For example, St. Ignatius in the contemplation on the Nativity of Jesus in the Spiritual Exercises suggests: "I will make myself a poor, little, unworthy servant, and as though present, look upon them, contemplate them, and serve them in their needs with all possible homage and reverence. Then I will reflect on myself that I may reap some fruit."

The Ignatian style of prayer can be utilized by all temperaments, although people of the SP and NT temperament may have some difficulty with this type of prayer. However, Ignatian Prayer best suits the SJ temperament (which Keirsey identifies with the Greek god Epimetheus[2]). Approximately 40 percent of the general population are of the SJ temperament.[3] From our observations in parishes during retreats and workshops, more than half of those in attendance at any church group meeting are apt to be of the SJ temperament. The SJ person has a very strong sense of duty and obligation, whether it be to God or to fellow human beings. Therefore, SJs are usually the people who continue going to church even though religion may lose its appeal for the other three temperaments.

The early development of the Christian Liturgical Year with its yearly commemorations of the events in the life of Jesus is a sign of the influence of SJ persons in the early Church; and the fact that Ignatian Prayer has been so popular down through the centuries may be explained by the preponderance of SJs among church-going persons. The best example of Ignatian Prayer in today's liturgy is the Liturgy of Holy Week. Beginning on Palm Sunday and carrying through to Easter Sunday, we commemorate in vivid detail each part of the Passion, Death, and Resurrection of Jesus. Those who participate in the Holy Week Services are taken back two thousand years and become a part of each event. From this participation some practical fruit for their present relationship with God and neighbor is drawn.

Characteristics of the SJ Temperament

The SJ persons have a deep sense of obligation and always want to feel useful. They want to be givers rather than receivers. Charity and service come easy to the SJ. They are deeply committed to caring for those in need and desire to contribute to the good of society. Very practical, they have a work ethic, with a strong sense of tradition and continuity with the past; and they like order and hierarchy in society. They want to belong to a group and like ceremonies and ritual. They have a strong sense of history and a great respect for elders and customs handed down from the past. They are the great conservators and stabilizers of society. Incapable of refusing responsibility they are often over-worked. "If I don't do it, who will?" Suspicious of change except when clearly necessary they usually opt for the status quo and are conservative in their tastes and choices. They are great law and order people; for them titles are important, and the law is important. They are careful, cautious, thorough, accurate, and industrious. They make good administrators and take deadlines seriously. They will do routine jobs without protest as long as these tasks have value and meaning. They show a common-sense, practical approach to everything and may be said to live by the Boy Scout motto: "Always be prepared." They are the most conscientious of all the temperaments. They represent all the positive qualities of the traditional phlegmatic temperament.

Many SJ persons lean toward pessimism, firmly believing in Murphy's law that if something can go wrong, it surely will. They tend to look on the dark side of life and to be prophets of doom and gloom. Therefore, they need to work at developing hope and trust to enable them to look on the bright side and become more optimistic. Persons of the other temperaments, especially the NFs, can help the SJs develop and deepen their hope and trust.

From what we know of St. James, the leader of the conservative element in the apostolic church, he was a typical SJ. He insisted that Christianity should keep faithful to the ancient traditions of the Jews. St. Matthew's Gospel is a typical SJ document with its emphasis on law and order and its stress on Jesus as the new Moses, the law-giver of the New Covenant. Matthew is also the Evangelist who constantly quotes texts from the Old Testament to show how Jesus is a continuation of the traditions handed down from the past.

Among the four dimensions of the Eucharist – Commemoration, Celebration, Anticipation, and Contemplation – the first dimension, Commemoration, appeals most to the SJ person. The homilist at Sunday worship should include the dimension of tradition and the history of salvation in every homily since it may be that somewhere around half of the congregation on an average Sunday will be SJs. It is also suggested that every Liturgy Committee be mindful of the liturgical year and celebrate and commemorate the past events of the history of salvation in a way to reach and touch the SJs.

Ignatian Spirituality

The spirituality of the SJ Ignatian temperament is a carefully organized regimen of striving toward a relationship with God. In a sense Ignatian spirituality is the opposite of Franciscan spirituality which depends upon spontaneity and openness to the Spirit. SJ persons prefer an orderly, well-planned agenda to follow and become upset when too many changes are suddenly introduced. Characteristically, SJs are militant in their opposition to the possibility of heresy and are strong in their fidelity to tradition.

As the historical dimension of the Christian faith is especially important for the SJ persons, they need to see the continuity between what we believe and practice today with what has been believed and practiced during the past twenty centuries of Christianity. If they can see the journey of faith as a spiral which again and again comes back to the same spot but each time at a higher level, the spirituality of the SJ person will be much enriched. They need the experience of both continuity with the past and new growth toward a previously selected goal. Mere adherence to the past leads to a static status quo where there is no promise of healthy advancement of any kind. A vibrant Ignatian spirituality, with its tendency toward intellectualism, will find a way to keep a good balance between all the values of the past and the new insights and graces that God wishes to pour out upon us each new day.

The concept that life is a part of a long journey of faith which began with the coming of Jesus to earth and which will continue until his return at the end of time is very much appreciated by the SJ temperament. SJs experience the history of salvation in the present by using their sense perceptions and sensible imagination to provide them with passage into the mysteries of Christ's life through the reading of the Scriptures. The SJ person employs his senses to relive in imagination and by observation the Scripture stories and then with his own innate sense of duty follows the admonition of Ignatius "to draw some practical fruit" by his service to others.

Ignatian spirituality is probably best expressed in the celebration of the Liturgical Year. Through the annual celebration of the events of the life, death, and resurrection of Jesus during the Church year, Christians not only commemorate the past events of history but actually make them present and operative for us today. This practice of celebrating the marvelous deeds of salvation history and remembering our covenant grows from the Jewish *Barakah*, prayers of thanksgiving, blessings, praises, and remembering. This practice is especially understood and appreciated by SJ persons. Gratitude for past benefits is very much a part of the SJ temperament, and liturgical piety is an appropriate example of Ignatian spirituality.

Ignatian Prayer

The purpose of Ignatian Prayer is to try to make the Gospels and the Scripture scenes become so alive and real to us that we can make a personal application of the teaching or message contained therein. Therefore, in addition to *commemoration*, the other key word for this type of prayer is *projection*. We attempt to project ourselves into the original events so that we become a part of them.

The sensible imagination is used more fully in Ignatian prayer than in any other type of prayer. Ignatius suggests that we try to use all five senses during our imaginary journey back to the events of salvation history and into the life of Jesus. We should try to imagine not only what we would see but also what each of the characters involved would say, what the wood of the cross would feel like, the smells, and even the tastes presented (for example, of the bitter gall and sour wine given to Jesus).

The purpose behind the insistence of St. Ignatius on this vivid recall of past events is to try to make the event as real as possible. We project ourselves back into the event and become a part of it. This does not mean that we necessarily project ourselves into the original characters but simply imagine ourselves as we now are but a part of the original event. By participating as affectively as possible, we are to draw some practical fruit for application to our present-day situation. For example, in the parable of the Good Samaritan (Luke 10:25-37), one might imagine oneself in place of the priest who passes by on the other side of the road lest he become involved; or we could make another meditation using the Ignatian method to think of ourselves as the man who fell among the robbers. Or, we can think of ourselves as the good Samaritan. We try to imagine what we might say to each of the characters in the Gospel story and what they might say to us.

Another way of using Ignatian Prayer is to put ourselves in the place of the different people who came to Jesus to be healed. Instead of thinking of physical ailments, we might think of ourselves as being spiritually blind, spiritually deaf, spiritually paralyzed, or covered with the leprosy of sin, etc. We can imagine ourselves coming to Jesus, or being brought to Jesus, and then having him reach out, touch us, and heal our spiritual malady. Our imagination can make this very vivid, and with sufficient faith on our part, we can indeed experience a true spiritual healing as a result of this prayer. The events in the life of Jesus can become so alive and real that we experience the presence of Jesus here and now in our midst. Such an encounter with God is the purpose of Ignatian prayer.

In addition to making ample use of the sensible imagination, Ignatian Prayer is very structured and orderly. Altogether ten distinct points are given by Ignatius for each of the meditations. They are:

1. Choice of topic
2. Preparatory prayer
3. Composition of place
4. Petition for special grace needed
5. See and reflect
6. Listen and reflect
7. Consider and reflect
8. Draw some practical fruit
9. Colloquy with God the Father, Jesus Christ, and the Blessed Mother
10. Closing with the "Our Father"

After the meditation, our feelings are aroused to make a proper response to the presence of Jesus. This corresponds to the Oratio part of *Lectio Divina.* Then, we take time just to be quiet and experience any new insights that our Intuitive Function might present to us. Thus, all four steps of *Lectio Divina* are practiced during Ignatian Prayer and all four functions utilized.

Problems in Using Ignatian Prayer

Unless they have been trained and experienced in this way of praying and thinking, many SJ persons, as well as others, find it difficult. In the past the SJ person was content to use vocal prayers[4] and traditional forms of prayer. Since the use of sensible imagination has not been popularly taught and practiced in our churches for the past several centuries, many people, even the SJs, often find Ignatian Prayer difficult to master. However, once one becomes familiar with the method and has sufficiently developed and exercised one's imagination, most SJs will come to depend upon this type of prayer as their regular, daily method of praying.

Since the SJ is inclined to be pessimistic, frequent meditation or reflection on the Resurrection of Jesus rather than constant recall of the Passion and Death is recommended to the SJ. In the *Spiritual Exercises of St. Ignatius* an attempt is made to strike a balance between the positive and the negative. Equal time, a whole week, is given to the Resurrection as to the Passion and Death. However, the characteristic note of gloom and doom is found in the emphasis by St. Ignatius on sin, judgment, and hell throughout the first week of the *Spiritual Exercises.*

Another problem some encounter using Ignatian Prayer is its tightly organized structure. Persons with a strong "P" temperament may rebel against the structure. Therefore, if they use Ignatian Prayer, it is recommended they change the order or omit any of the parts that do not appeal to them. However, persons with a strong "J" temperament usually take to Ignatian Prayer like a duck to water.

The SP temperament especially finds this tightly organized structure difficult to follow. People who have not been able to put order into their daily lives will probably have a hard time remembering the different steps of Ignatian Prayer. It is like learning to drive a car with a stick shift: The first time is difficult; but after a period of learning, it becomes second nature. Furthermore, adequate time must be allocated to the prayer exercise. We must not try to hurry the process, otherwise nothing happens and no value is derived from this form of prayer. Help from a leader trained in conducting the Spiritual Exercises will be very beneficial in making these Gospel scenes come alive.[5]

15 Ignatian-Type Prayer Suggestions

The Ignatian Method is to place oneself in the Biblical scene and to become a part of it by way of imagination. Ignatius suggests that we try to imagine what we might see, what we might hear, and what the persons in the scene might be doing. Always, at each point of the contemplation, Ignatius says, we must "try to draw some practical fruit from the reflection for our own life today." In other words, what changes or challenges does our reflection on the event furnish us? Infusing the following prayer suggestions, it is suggested that one use either the four steps of *Lectio Divina* or the ten points recommended by St. Ignatius.

~ Prayer Suggestion 1 ~

Read Luke 10:38–42

Imagine yourself a friend and fellow-villager of either Mary, Martha, or Lazarus. You happen to meet one of them in the village and you are told that Jesus of Nazareth is coming to visit in Bethany. You express an interest in meeting him, and you are invited to come the next evening to have dinner with them and Jesus.

Close your eyes and try to relive in your imagination, with as many vivid details as you can, what your meeting and the ensuing conversation with Jesus would be like. Draw some practical fruit from it.

~ Prayer Suggestion 2 ~

You, a devout Israelite from Ephesus, are a stranger in Jerusalem on your first trip for the Passover. It is Good Friday morning; you find yourself caught up in a noisy crowd leading a man away to be crucified. You have never seen a crucifixion, so out of curiosity you follow the crowd to Calvary and find the man's name is Jesus of Nazareth. You are fascinated by the proceedings and by the conduct of Jesus. You stay until he dies. Close your eyes and in your imagination relive the scene and try to capture the impressions and conclusions you may have experienced. Draw some spiritual fruit for your own spiritual growth. What change is this experience going to make in your life?

~ Prayer Suggestion 3~

Read Luke 24:13–35

You are one of the two disciples on the road to Emmaus on Easter Sunday afternoon. Close your eyes after reading the Scripture passage and try to relive the whole scene from beginning to end. Draw some spiritual fruit from the experience. For example, invite Jesus to stay with you: "The day is nearly over. The night is at hand. Stay with us."

~ Prayer Suggestion 4 ~

Read John 21:1–19

Imagine that you are Peter. Read the story very carefully so that you will remember all of the details. Then close your eyes and relive the scene in your imagination. Try to capture your feelings when Jesus asks you three times, "Do you love me?" Then answer the way you would want to answer rather than merely repeat what Peter said. When Jesus tells you: "Follow me," try to imagine what that might mean in the immediate future of your present life.

~ Prayer Suggestion 5 ~

Read Luke 10:25–37

Read the parable of the Good Samaritan and try to imagine yourself, first of all, as the priest who passes by on the other side of the road. What reasons could you give for refusing to get involved? Then try to imagine yourself as the person who fell among the robbers and who was left half-dead by the side of the road. What might you think as you see people pass you by and refuse your cries for help? Thirdly, imagine yourself as the Good Samaritan. Try to envision some situations today where you could act as a Good Samaritan to others in trouble.

~ Prayer Suggestion 6 ~

Read Mark 9:14–29

Read the story. Imagine yourself as the father of the possessed boy and apply the conversation between Jesus and the father to your own situation. Instead of an afflicted son, imagine the affliction is some fault of yours which has resisted cure. Bring this affliction to Jesus and ask him to cure it.

~ Prayer Suggestion 7 ~

Read Luke 7:36–50

Imagine yourself as the penitent woman who comes to Jesus in the house of Simon the Pharisee, washes his feet with her tears, and dries them with her hair. Try to imagine why you should be weeping and how you came to be convinced that Jesus would understand and show mercy. Imagine your reaction when you hear him saying to you, "Many sins are forgiven you because you have loved much."

~ Prayer Suggestion 8~

Read Luke 4:1–13

Put yourself in the place of Jesus, imagine yourself being tempted in the same way as Jesus. How might you respond? The temptations of Jesus are suggestions that he misuse his newly-received powers to serve himself rather than use them for the benefit of others. He could change water into wine for the benefit of a newly married couple, or multiply loaves and fishes to feed a hungry multitude in the wilderness, but he must not change stones into bread for his own use. Similarly, he could walk on water and calm the storms at sea for the benefit of others, but he must not cast himself down from the pinnacle of the temple to show off his power over nature. He could use his power over people to teach them about the Kingdom of God but never to make himself their king and ruler. We too have been given special powers. We must not use them for our benefit but always to help others. What can we do to make sure we follow Jesus's example when we are tempted to abuse the power God gives us?

~ Prayer Suggestion 9~

Read Mark 8:27–38

Jesus's Galilean Crisis: Jesus is half-way through his public ministry. The people are beginning to abandon him (John 6:66). The Pharisees and religious authorities are plotting his death. Everything for which he has been working seems lost. Jesus leaves Galilee and goes into the pagan territory of Decapolis. He becomes aware that Isaiah 53 foretells his fate. He is seriously tempted to run away from his vocation. When he shares this with the apostles, Peter tries to dissuade Jesus: "God forbid that any such thing happens to you." Jesus turns on Peter in anger: "Get behind me, you adversary. You are trying to make me trip and fall. You are not judging by God's standards but by man's" (Matt 16:22-23). Put yourself in the place of Jesus or Peter. How would you react in a similar situation? What can you do to accept more willingly the crosses and disappointments in your present life?

~ Prayer Suggestion 10 ~

Read Mark 14:32–42

Agony in the Garden: Jesus is still struggling with the destiny to which his Heavenly Father has called him. "O Abba, you have the power to do all things. Take away this cup of suffering from me." He looks for comfort and sympathy from Peter, James, and John but finds them asleep. Identify with Jesus in his agony. Recall some instances in your own life when you felt abandoned both by God and your friends. Through this identity with Jesus you will find the grace and strength to abandon yourself to God: "Not my will but thine be done."

~ Prayer Suggestion 11~

Read Mark 10:46–52

Think of yourself as the blind Bartimaeus who hears that Jesus of Nazareth is passing. "Jesus, Son of David, have pity on me!" Jesus calls you over and asks: "What do you want me to do for you?" "Rabboni, I want to see." "Be on your way, your faith has healed you." We all are spiritually blind. We so often miss the obvious.

We are blind to the needs of others. We are blind to our own faults and sins. Say to Jesus, "Rabboni, I want to see." Jesus lays his hands on you and you experience healing. Your eyes are opened, and you see that to which you had previously been blind.

~ Prayer Suggestion 12~

Read Mark 10:17–31

Imagine yourself the rich young man who asks Jesus, "What more can I do?" Jesus hears your request and challenges you to go and dispose of everything you own, and give it to the poor, and then come and follow him. Would you have the courage to do this if you knew Jesus were asking this of you? Or would you turn away like the rich young man because you are still attached to the things of this world? It is hard to say whether we would act like the rich young man or like Peter who exclaims: "We have put aside everything to follow you!" But by using our imagination to project ourselves back into this Gospel scene, we should be able to discern where we now stand. Then, pray for the grace to follow Peter.

~ Prayer Suggestion 13 ~

Read Luke 15:11–32

Read the story of the Prodigal Son; try to place yourself in turn as the younger son, as the elder brother, and then as the father. Try to think of times in your life when you have acted as each of the three characters.

What opportunity might you have in your present life to follow the example of the father of the prodigal son?

~ Prayer Suggestion 14 ~

Read Luke 16:19–31

Let us put ourselves in the place of the rich man in the story. Think of times when we have passed by the beggars who lay at our gate. Think of the times we have feasted sumptuously while half of the world's population starved. "Remember that you were well off in your lifetime, while Lazarus was in misery. Now he has found consolation here, but you have found torment." God forbid that we will ever have to hear these words from our Lord and Judge. What do we need to change to avoid hearing these words? To make this change of heart more real, try to relive as vividly as possible the Gospel parable to the very end, imagining that you are the rich man who has neglected Lazarus the beggar.

~ Prayer Suggestion 15 ~

Read Luke 18:9–14

Put yourself in turn in the places of the Pharisee and the Publican. Does your ordinary prayer resemble that of the Pharisee or of the Publican? What changes are needed to make your prayer more in accord with the teachings of Jesus and the example of the Publican? Imagine yourself as the Pharisee standing in the front of the church on a Sunday morning praising and thanking God that you are not like the rest of the people or like some poor wretches you know. Does this resemble any experiences in your own life? Does your prayer ever fall into the category of the prayer of the Pharisee? How can you become more like the Publican?

CHAPTER FIVE

AUGUSTINIAN PRAYER & SPIRITUALITY: *THE NF TEMPERAMENT*

In this book we have given the name Augustinian to a very popular type of prayer which appeals especially to the NF temperament. St. Augustine, in whose honor it is named, was likely an NF (Intuitive-Feeler). One of the best known of the early Christian Fathers of the Church, he developed rules of spirituality for the monasteries of monks and convents of virgins in North Africa. These became models for the rules and constitutions of the majority of religious congregations of Western Christianity. The Augustinian method of prayer and spirituality was adopted and used by the Fathers of the Church and many other spiritual masters down through the centuries. The long history of usage and success of this type of prayer is probably due to the fact that the majority of the canonized saints seem to be of the NF temperament.

In Ignatian Prayer, where the key word is *projection,* one is projected back into the biblical scene by using the sensible imagination to become affectively a part of the original event and then to draw some practical fruit for our life today. The key word to describe Augustinian Prayer is *transposition*. In Augustinian Prayer, one uses creative imagination[1] to transpose the words of Sacred Scripture to our situation today. One tries to imagine (intuit) what meaning the words of Scripture would have if Jesus Christ, or God the Father, or the Holy Spirit appeared and spoke them to us at this moment.

In Augustinian Prayer, we try to think of the words of the Bible as though they were a personal letter from God addressed to each one of us. Only secondarily are we concerned about the original, historical meaning of a text of Scripture; our primary concern during Augustinian Prayer is trying to discern what meaning these revealed words have for us today. Thus, the Word of God becomes alive and applicable to our situation. For example, consider the words God addressed to the people of Israel in Isaiah 43, and imagine they are being spoken to you now: "Thus says the Lord who created you and formed you: 'Fear not, for I have redeemed you; I have called you by name, you are mine… You are precious in my eyes and glorious, and I love you… fear not, for I am with you.'"

Transposing the ancient words of the Bible to the situation of the present is a practice that goes back to New Testament times. Jesus himself transposed the words of the Hebrew prophets to the situation of his own time. The Gospel narrators, St. Paul, and the other New Testament writers used transposition to apply the words of the Old Testament to the situations of the first century of the Christian Era. The Church Fathers of both the East and the West used this method of updating the Bible to find a way to relate its meaning to their time.

Throughout the course of Christian history, saints, mystics, spiritual masters, spiritual writers, preachers, and just ordinary persons have used this method of transposition to discover the meaning of God's word and God's will for themselves. While all temperaments find Augustinian Prayer meaningful and helpful, those of the NF temperament are usually the most adept in using it. The NF person has the most highly developed Intuition and Feeling, which are the two psychological functions most used in this type of prayer. Sensation and Thinking are also used, but to catch the new insights applicable to ourselves in the words of Scripture the intuitive powers are especially needed. To personalize the message the Feeling Function must be activated; otherwise the words remain abstract and impersonal and will have no lasting effect upon our lives. Since the Dominant and Auxiliary Functions of the NF person are Intuition and Feeling, they usually find the greatest joy and benefit from using Augustinian Prayer.

Characteristics of the NF Temperament

NF persons are usually creative, optimistic, verbal, persuasive, outspoken, good at both writing and speaking (Keirsey compares the NF with the Greek god Apollo[2]). They have a great need for self-expression and communicate with others easily. NFs are good listeners, good at counselling, good in resolving conflicts and making peace. They dislike conflict and have difficulty operating at peak efficiency when the situation becomes tense and strained. They like to have face-to-face encounters and are able to read faces and catch non-verbal communications. NFs have deep feelings and may be upset if treated impersonally. They find it difficult to handle negative criticism, and become discouraged when meeting a negative attitude in others, but blossom under affirmation. They freely give and need strokes and communicate their own enthusiasm to others. They need acceptance, support, and prefer cooperation rather than competition.

NFs are highly committed to helping others and usually relate well to those who befriend them. They are enthusiastic, insightful, full of empathy, understanding, and compassion. They see in others possibilities for good that other temperaments do not perceive. Being person-oriented they are apt to have favorites; but persons are always more important than things. Because Thinking and Sensing are their Inferior Functions, NFs must make a special effort to be logical and correct in their thinking and to be aware of details and routine.

NFs are always searching for meaning, authenticity, self-identity. They have a great urge for perfection and wholeness and are quite idealistic. They have a hunger for integrity and are willing to make great sacrifices to attain it. Personal growth and development are necessities for both themselves and anyone for whom they feel a responsibility. They are the natural rescuers of those in trouble, and this leads to the danger of becoming too involved in others' problems. Both the giving and receiving of spiritual direction are high in priority for them. Therefore, the NFs usually make good spiritual directors who help others grow in spirituality and wholeness. Even though NFs are only about 12 percent of the total population,[3] a much larger percentage of NFs make retreats, frequent houses of prayer, and write about prayer and spirituality. Self-improvement, self-development, self-actualization are the top of their priorities. NFs have a tremendous hunger and thirst for growth in their inner life; and for those who believe in God, this can be satisfied only in prayer, spiritual reading, contemplation. They experience a great need for periods of quiet and silence in order to connect with their inner selves. "How can I become the person that I am supposed to be?" and "How can I become truly real, authentic, and true to my own unique self?" are questions uppermost in the mind of the NF. NFs are happy and content only when they are convinced that their outer life is in harmony with their inner self.[4]

Contrasted with the SJs who can be pessimistic about themselves and others, NFs usually are optimistic and able to see good in everyone. Because of their optimism and hope, they will make personal sacrifices to help others grow and find their way in life. The NF, like the NT, has that sixth sense which we call Intuition. This makes them capable of seeing possibilities and potentials to which the SJ and SP may be blind. Sometimes this is expressed as a psychic ability or as Extra Sensory Perception (ESP).

NFs will enter into a life-long process of "becoming" yet may never reach the ideal of "being". As intuitives, they are never content with the present but always striving to fulfill the unlimited potential for growth that God has implanted in every one of us. A great urge for truth, beauty, purity, perfection, and wholeness is theirs; and they often set such high goals for themselves that they are unable to attain them. Because the NF is future-oriented, while the majority of people (the 80 percent who are either SJ or SP) are present-oriented, other temperaments often have a hard time understanding the NF's dissatisfaction with the present and their constant desire for change.

Augustinian Spirituality

The NF needs to find meaning in everything. The NF wants to know that what one does makes a difference; that each person can make a unique contribution; that they are important; that God loves each one of us unconditionally, as we are now, sins and all. The NF needs to be assured of this every day in order to keep growing into a deeper and more intimate relationship with God. Experiencing a personal relationship with God is the one essential element of any authentic NF spirituality. Therefore, daily prayer and quiet are a must for persons of this temperament.

The NF derives a heightened sense of meaning from every event and relationship by constantly seeking the hidden meaning of things. Through Intuition and creative imagination, the NF is able to give new meaning to life's experiences, a meaning beyond the mere external event of the here and now. Whatever is actually present is never quite sufficient for the NF. Totally untenable for the NF is the thought that the visible, external, here-and-now thing or event is all there is. There always has to be something better on the horizon, or around the corner, if only one will search for it. Invariably this "better" thing will be something of the inner world of the spirit. Hence, the hunger and thirst for God and prayer that most NFs experience.

Just as the SJ (Ignatian) temperament has a profound interest in the past, the NF temperament has a keen interest in future possibilities. NFs are the visionaries of the world. Persons of the NF temperament try to anticipate new directions into which destiny and the will of God are leading them and the world. From this temperament usually come the prophets who seek to read the signs of the times. NFs are the eschatological

Christians who are open to the gifts of the Holy Spirit; and the dimension of *anticipation* is the part of the liturgy which appeals most to them.

Because the NF is always reading between the lines in order to catch the inexpressible, the spiritual, the hidden meaning, this temperament best understands symbols[5] and their use in prayer and liturgy. Symbols are the way God speaks to us; and we, to God. Since the full meaning and experience of God are limited by external signs or words, symbols are the touchstones which we use to reach a greater understanding of these realities.

The parables of Jesus in the Gospel describing God and the Kingdom of God are symbolic ways to illuminate something that cannot be literally expressed in human words. The NF, and the NT, with their strong and creative Intuition, best understand symbols; while the SJ and the SP, because they always want to be literal and factual, even with God, frequently have a harder time with symbols. By catching and meditating on the symbols that appear in a prayer period, God and the work of the Spirit become more real and meaningful for the NF. New insights into the nature of God and the relationship between God and oneself are thus attained. The NF's faith commitment is thereby enhanced and strengthened.

A great many of the books on prayer found on the market today are written by NF persons and addressed especially to the NF temperament. Therefore, of all the four basic temperaments, the NFs are usually the best cared for spiritually; but they also need this special care, since without spiritual growth and development they wither, fade, and die just like a plant that is not watered, nourished, and tended.

Augustinian Prayer

Of all the temperaments, the NF needs more time in prayer and quiet meditation than any of the others. For the NF such time is not a luxury but a necessity as far as personal development and relationship with God are concerned. In prayer the NF will use all four functions of Sensing, Intuition, Thinking, and Feeling; but their Intuition and Feeling are used most. Never content with the superficial, external meaning of a Scripture passage or other spiritual reading, they constantly search for the fuller, richer meaning. "What do these words of Scripture mean to me in my present situation?" "What message is the Lord trying to convey to me in these ancient words of the Bible?" By using their Intuition in this transposition, the NF makes the Bible relevant to current personal and community problems and needs. Then the Feeling Function, activated by the grace of the Holy Spirit, personalizes and ratifies this newly discovered meaning for incorporation into one's life.

In order to practice the Prayer of Transposition, which we call Augustinian Prayer, the NF needs to open themselves to their creative imagination. Believing as we do that the biblical writers were able to penetrate the wisdom of God and bring a portion of this eternal wisdom down to earth, our Intuitive Function and our creative imagination are used to discover how to apply this wisdom to our situation. Since the wisdom of God is eternal and applicable to all ages and all situations, the NF transposition of the message of the Bible to the needs of the present generation has been a way of praying down through the ages. Such openness to the Holy Spirit involves a certain amount of risk and experimentation which should always be subject to continued discernment. Therefore, a spiritual journal, where thoughts and inspirations are recorded, is a great help to the NF not only in making the transposition of meaning to today's situation but also for reviewing the progress and validity of one's insights or inspirations. Usually good with words, both in speaking and writing, the NFs find journal keeping not a chore but a joy. They use the journal to discover the deeper meanings of life and to experience new spiritual growth. NFs agree with Cardinal Newman, who once said that he could pray best at the point of a pen.

To be fully effective, Augustinian Prayer should consist of a dialogue between God and oneself. This can best be accomplished by using the four steps of *Lectio Divina*. First, we listen attentively to what God is telling us in the words of Scripture by endeavoring to read between the lines to discern the deeper meaning contained therein. Second, we reflect prayerfully upon their meaning and try to apply this eternal wisdom to our situation today. Third, we respond to God's word by appropriate personal feelings and dialogue. Finally, we remain quiet and still in order to be open to any new insights that our Intuitive faculty brings forth. The NF person will probably spend the most time on the last two parts of the prayer, wherein their Dominant and Auxiliary Functions of Feeling and Intuition are activated. For the NF temperament this type of prayer comes very naturally and quite easily. Other temperaments, when using Augustinian Prayer, may need to use more psychic energy to activate their Intuitive and Feeling Functions; therefore, we suggest that they should be well-rested and allow ample time for this type of prayer.

Since the life of the NF revolves around personal relationships, this will also be true in the NF's prayer life. The

NF should endeavor to create a good, loving relationship with each person of the Trinity: a parental relationship with the First Person; a brotherly, friendly relationship with Jesus; a spousal relationship of love with the Holy Spirit. Saints may also serve as models for the NF, and reading the lives of holy, mature, self-actualized persons who have had a good relationship with God will help to foster a growth of love for God in the NF. Ikons, statues, and other representations of art, which express beautifully and symbolically a good relationship with God will also help the NF in prayer.

15 Augustinian-Type Prayer Suggestions

~ Prayer Suggestion 1 ~

Read Isaiah 43:1–5

Change the words "Jacob" and "Israel" to your own first name. Try to imagine the Lord speaking these words directly to you. What meaning would they have for you in your present situation? Try to transpose the message from God to yourself today. What is the Lord talking about when He tells you, "Fear not"? What fears do you have? Water and fire were the two great dangers which aroused the fears of ancient people; what are the greatest dangers you face in your life? What is the Lord telling you to do in time of danger? Imagine Jesus saying to you now, "You are precious in my eyes, and I love you." "Fear not, I am with you." How do you see this to be true in your own situation today?

~ Prayer Suggestion 2 ~

Read Hosea 2:16–22

Imagine God or Jesus speaking these words to you. What meaning would you derive from them? Change the words, pronouns, names, so that they apply to your present situation; and write the passage on a piece of paper. Imagine going to the mail-box and receiving today a personal letter addressed to you containing these words. What meaning would they have?

~ Prayer Suggestion 3 ~

Read John 17

Rewrite the whole chapter of St. John's gospel so that it could be a prayer that Jesus might be praying for you personally at this very moment in your life. Change or omit whatever words or verses that do not apply to you. If you have a tape recorder, read the new prayer into it. Then listen to it. Close your eyes and imagine Jesus praying thusly for you today. Or, you might simply read it slowly to yourself; and imagine Jesus praying or speaking these words to you.

Prayer Suggestion 4

Read Ephesians 3:14–21

Using the prayer, change the pronouns from the second person (you) to the first person (me). Write out the new prayer so that it is a prayer for yourself. Then read it aloud several times. Recite it slowly; put as much meaning into the words as you can. Try to savor every word and phrase. What changes in your present attitudes does this prayer suggest to you?

~ Prayer Suggestion 5 ~

Read John 14:1–16

Close your eyes after reading this passage and try to imagine Jesus speaking these words to you. What would they mean to you? Repeat those words of Jesus that have special value for you; savor them lovingly, joyfully. Try writing them down in your journal in order to impress them more deeply on your mind and memory.

~ Prayer Suggestion 6 ~

Read Matthew 5:38–48

Read the passage slowly several times. Try to discern what meaning the words might have if spoken by Jesus to you at this very moment. Whom do you need to forgive? How might Jesus be asking you today to turn the other cheek, to go the extra mile, to give away your shirt as well as your cloak? Feel free to apply these words of Jesus to some other area of life besides material possessions.

~ Prayer Suggestion 7 ~

Read Isaiah 54:4–14

Read the passage slowly a few times. Try to imagine God the Father saying these words to you. What meaning might they have?

~ Prayer Suggestion 8 ~

Read Philippians 3:7–16

Put yourself in the place of a person in Philippi who received this letter from Paul. He is writing with you specifically in mind. He knows your situation quite well. How do the words apply to you?

~ Prayer Suggestion 9 ~

Read Isaiah 58:2–14

Justice and charity to the poor are the most authentic forms of fasting. How far can these words of God apply to your life? What more can you do to share your bread with the hungry, shelter the oppressed and the homeless, clothe the naked? Try to imagine God saying these words to you today. What is He asking of you at this time in your life?

~ Prayer Suggestion 10 ~

Read Micah 6:8

"You have been told, O man, what is good and what the Lord requires of you: Do right, love goodness, and walk humbly with your God." Consider how these three requests sum up your relationship with God and your fellow human beings. Imagine God speaking these words to you. Close your eyes and repeat them slowly over and over again. Try to apply them to your own situation. What is God asking of you?

~ Prayer Suggestion 11 ~

Read Matthew 7:1–5

Imagine Jesus speaking these words to you today. How far do they apply? What is he asking of you? What changes is he asking you to make in your life?

~ Prayer Suggestion 12 ~

Read Matthew 18:21–35

"My heavenly Father will treat you in exactly the same way unless each of you forgives his brother from his heart." Think of the persons in your life who have hurt you by what they said, or did, or failed to say and do. Taking them one by one, try to forgive each one in your heart and pray for them. Do this again and again even though you may have already done it in the past.

~ Prayer Suggestion 13 ~

Read John 8:1–11

"Has no one condemned you?" "No one, Lord." "Neither do I condemn you. Go now and sin no more." Think of the faults you still have, consider them one by one. Think of the things that others criticize and find fault with you. Imagine them bringing you to Jesus to have him condemn you. Instead he says to you: "Neither do I condemn you. Go, sin no more." How would this make you feel?

~ Prayer Suggestion 14 ~

Read Matthew 25:31–46

"What you do to the least of my brethren, you do unto me." Who are the "least brethren" in your life? Who are the people whom you consider beneath you? Alcoholics, drug abusers, welfare recipients, conservatives/liberals?[6] Mother Teresa of Calcutta speaks of the presence of Jesus in the "distressing disguise of the poor." What should you do or say in regard to them if you see Christ in each one of them?

~ Prayer Suggestion 15 ~

Read I Corinthians 13:4-8

"Love is never rude or self-seeking. There is no limit to its forbearance, no limit to its trust, its hope, its endurance." This is an ideal for which we must continually strive. Talk to Jesus about your failures in charity and ask him what he wants you to do. Put your own name in the passage each time the word "love" or "charity" is used. How authentic would such words be in your regard? What do you need to change to make them authentic?

CHAPTER SIX

FRANCISCAN PRAYER
& SPIRITUALITY:
THE SP TEMPERAMENT

In the thirteenth century St. Francis of Assisi introduced a type of spirituality which is ideal for the SP (Sensing-Perceiving) temperament. St. Francis, who was probably an ESFP, exhibited all of the marks of the SP temperament, which is characterized by an attitude of openness and willingness to go in any direction that the Spirit calls.

Since we seem to be living in an age of the kind of individualism typical of the SP, it is not surprising that a large number of those taking part in the Prayer Project during 1982 chose Franciscan Prayer as their favorite way of prayer. This was despite the fact that less than ten percent of those participating in the Project were of the SP temperament. About 30 percent of the general population of this country belong to the SP temperament.[1] Hence, understanding this type and learning how to use and utilize Franciscan Prayer will be beneficial to a large number of people.

Characteristics of the SP Temperament

SPs must be free, unconfined, and able to do whatever their inner spirit moves them to do (Keirsey identifies SPs with the Greek god Dionysus[2]). Therefore, it is important that the SP be dedicated to God so that this inner spirit is the Holy Spirit and not a merely human spirit or an evil spirit. SPs are impulsive and dislike being tied down by rules. They want to follow whatever impulse strikes them. Again, it is important that they be committed to doing God's will; otherwise, their free spirit can lead them far astray.

SPs love action and become easily bored with the status quo. They are crisis-oriented, good at unsnarling messes, and able to get things moving. They make good trouble-shooters, negotiators, diplomats. They have unlimited energy as long as the crisis exists and work best and most efficiently when it is necessary to respond quickly and dramatically. They are flexible, easy to get along with, open-minded, adaptable, willing to change their position. They are good as conciliators since in their view almost everything is negotiable.

They live very much in the present without concern either for the past or future. Neither yesterday nor tomorrow exist for a thorough-going SP. They are always looking for something new: new places to go, new things to do. They dislike practice and want simply to perform and act. They thrive on excitement, adventure, risk, challenge. They hunger for activity and enjoyment. Optimistic, cheerful, light-hearted, witty, charming, they live life intensively and are capable of unrelenting vigor when challenged and excited.

The air takes on a glow when an SP enters the room. They bring with them a sense that something exciting is about to happen. They are good entertainers and are usually the life of a party with an array of stories. They live life extensively, are able to survive setbacks, and are only temporarily defeated.

Franciscan Spirituality

Franciscan spirituality is popular among those of action, those who want and need to do things for others. Acts of loving service can be a most effective form of prayer; yet so often we neglect to think of this showing of fraternal love as prayer. If an SP has made a commitment to centering their life in God and in the doing of God's will, all these acts will be accompanied by a free-flowing, spontaneous, informal praising, and loving dialogue with God. Franciscan spirituality is very optimistic and sees the beauty, goodness, and love of God everywhere.

The whole of God's creation is a Bible for the Franciscan temperament. God speaks to them through every sense impression: all that they see, or hear, or feel, or smell, or taste. Yet the books of the Bible, especially the Gospel accounts of the life of Jesus, will have a special appeal for the Sensing-Perceiving person. St. Francis of Assisi understood the true meaning of the Incarnation and the teachings and example of Jesus perhaps better than any other follower of Christ. When one considers that a Sensing-Perceiving person like St. Francis connects with God primarily through their sense impressions, it would follow that since the Incarnation is the visible, audible, tangible presence of God upon earth, the SP could relate quite well to Jesus's life and his teachings through the parables. Therefore, the Incarnation of God in the life of Jesus is the center around which Franciscan life and spirituality revolve and coalesce.

Because of their impetuosity and generosity, SPs are fond of the "grand gesture" whereby they dramatically express their commitment to God. A beautiful and humorous example of this is when Francis of Assisi stripped off his clothes in front of the bishop and handed them over to his father. There are numerous examples of these dramatic, impulsive actions in St. Francis' life and in the lives of other persons of the SP temperament.

Ordinarily, SPs are not excessively concerned about either the past or the future. They are usually merciful and forgiving toward the past and optimistic and hopeful about the future. Their motto is *carpe diem* (seize the day); but if they are centered in God, this will not be in the way of the Roman Epicureans but in following the teaching of Jesus: "Do not be concerned about tomorrow. It will have troubles enough of its own. Sufficient for the day is the trouble thereof" (Matt 6:34). Since they are often attracted to following a hero, they should take as their model Jesus Christ or St. Francis himself.

The SP does not respond well to the symbolic but is primarily interested in the real and literal. However, they are capable of great and heroic sacrifices for a worthy cause. Therefore, their generosity may result in untold sacrifices which other temperaments would be unable to endure. Once convinced of the value of a goal, the pursuit of it becomes play and not work for the SP temperament. The SP is willing to give up all ties to the present and wander off after some faraway ideal. Some of the most heroic and greatest saints, including St. Peter the Apostle and St. Mark, and many missionaries, show the characteristics of this temperament in their works and deeds.

Franciscan Prayer

Franciscan Prayer makes full use of the five senses and will be flexible and free-flowing. It is what we call "spirit-filled prayer," totally open to the presence and voice of the Holy Spirit present in each one of us. Since SP persons can see God in the whole of creation, they are able to make a fruitful meditation on the beauty of a flower, a meadow, a lake, a waterfall, a mountain, the ocean, or any event of nature such as sunrises and sunsets, the changes of the seasons – spring's new growth, fall's colors, winter's fresh snow. When considering the life of Jesus, SPs will be more concerned about events rather than His teachings. The events surrounding his birth, his hidden life, and his baptism; his miracles (feeding the multitude, walking on the water, supervising the miraculous catch of fish); and his passion, death, and resurrection will hold special interest for the SP. The parables Jesus uses are also apt to have a great appeal to the SP person.

If there is any temperament that can honestly claim that their work is their prayer, this would be the SP. Much of their prayer is what is called virtual prayer[3] or the prayer of good works. Of all the temperaments they have the least need for long periods of formal prayer. While other temperaments may need as much as a whole hour of prayer time each day, the SP person functions well with 20 to 30 minutes of formal prayer in the ordinary working day. Nevertheless, they should try to give at least the minimum of time aforementioned to formal prayer daily while endeavoring in their own fashion to live in the presence of God, and thus be united with Him, throughout the day.

A prayerful SP will find that the thought of God predominates every waking moment. The famous Jesus

Prayer: "Lord Jesus Christ, have mercy on me, a sinner" and other short, specific prayers are readily used by the SPs and enable them to live constantly in the presence of God and to see His hand in everything: in nature, in the events of divine providence, in other people, and in themselves. The Psalms, along with the Gospels, are usually the favorite Bible books of the SP. However, because of their enthusiastic nature which is so often filled with joy, praise, peace, and love, SPs should be encouraged to experiment with new forms and ways of praying which are not confined to the formal and traditional.

Since they usually have a great facility for spontaneous prayer, they may belong to a charismatic prayer group.[4] In addition to praise, the aspect of the sacred liturgy which appeals most to the SP is *celebration*. They love to celebrate the goodness, greatness, love, and power of God. Once again, we go back to the possibility that this is a Franciscan Age since we see our present liturgies called Celebrations rather than the Sacrifice of the Mass they were called in previous times.

The Sensing-Perceiving person dislikes formal prayer and prefers a free-flowing, informal communing with God. When an SP makes a directed or long retreat, the retreat director should give persons of this temperament the freedom to do whatever strikes them, indicating however that they should share with the director all that occurs between them and God in the course of the day. If forced to follow a strict routine, such as the Spiritual Exercises of the Ignatian Retreat, SPs may find it stifling or the routine so repressive that they will either quit and go home or feel miserable for the duration of the retreat. To force this temperament into a strict schedule or rigid routine of prayer is a waste of time and totally unproductive of spiritual fruit. The more freedom in their prayer time, the more fruitful it is apt to be.

Once SPs decide to give themselves totally to God, there is simply no sacrifice that they will refuse to make; but it has to be in accord with the SP temperament and not according to the SJ, NT, or NF way of praying and living. A spiritual director or retreat master who fails to understand this and tries to force the SP into the same mold that other temperaments follow will accomplish little or no good at all and probably do some harm. The SP may give up the pursuit of holiness or give up the guidance of a director who fails to make proper allowance for the peculiarities of the SP temperament.

The SPs are best at short-range projects. They need to see quick or instant results. Therefore, any spiritual exercise which will show some worthwhile fruit in a short time should be chosen for them and by them. For example, they might be given acts of charity and ministry to others on a short-term basis. Since they thrive on the visible, audible, and tangible, they love to work with their hands and with tools. During a retreat they may be given something which they can do with their hands: molding clay; painting a mandala; crocheting or knitting; making a banner; or executing some other work of art. By way of relaxation during a retreat, an SP might assist around the grounds by doing some gardening or other physical activity. This answers their need for action and for good works.

The SP loves to give and receive gifts and to see the reaction of pleasure and surprise in the receiver. They might be encouraged to use the arts and crafts to make things which can be given as gifts to others. At prayer, the SP will often show forth love for God by using a musical instrument, a paint brush, or anything that involves movement, action, and the senses. SPs have a strong appreciation of beauty and feel a need to produce beauty by their own efforts. St. Francis expressed this in the creation of the Christmas creche. Paper and pencil work is apt to be deadly and counter-productive for the SP, so a spiritual journal is not to be recommended. To relax, the SP needs some less demanding activity like walking in the woods and taking time to observe and reflect upon the sights and sounds of nature.

Since the SP cannot tolerate long periods of silence, strict adherence to the 30-Day Ignatian Spiritual Exercises is not recommended for this temperament. Inconsideration of their special needs, the rules for such a retreat need to be bent. If more than one SP is attending the retreat, they should be permitted to have periods of conversation together but not with the other retreatants. If they opt to follow the silence of the retreat, some challenge should be given them: a difficult goal which will be productive of short-term, noticeable results. If it is challenging enough, the SP will spend untold hours of continuous perseverance on it.

A goal that might be suggested to the SP during a retreat or in spiritual direction would be that they strive to have the thought and will of God predominate every waking moment of the day so that they can see the hand of God in everything that happens. Once convinced of the value of such a goal, the SP will give themselves no rest until it is attained.

15 Franciscan-Type Prayer Suggestions

The SP person may or may not find it useful to follow the four steps of *Lectio Divina*. However, when other temperaments use these SP prayer suggestions, it is recommended that the four steps of *Lectio Divina* be used.

~ Prayer Suggestion 1 ~

Read I Cor. 1:23–25; Gal 6:14; Phil 2:5–8; Isaiah 52:12 to 53:13

Take your crucifix, look intently at it, feel it, kiss it. In your imagination go back to the first Good Friday. Try to put yourself in the place of Jesus being nailed to the cross. This is what St. Francis did in the cave at Alverno near the end of his life. As a result, he experienced the Stigmata, the actual wounds of Jesus, in his hands and feet. Try to imagine having the nails driven through your wrists and feet; try to feel the kind of stabbing pain Jesus must have felt. Try to identify with Jesus in his passion and crucifixion. Imagine yourself hanging suspended on the cross for three long hours, stripped of your clothing, naked before the jeering mob of people, wearing the crown of thorns, suffering in every pore of your body, suspended between heaven and earth.

Why this terrible pain and agony? Why this waste of human life? Jesus offered himself as a victim of love, offered himself to the forces of evil which were threatening to engulf the world at the time. Imagine these immense forces of evil as a giant river in flood stage sweeping across the face of the earth and destroying everything in its path. Jesus offered his fragile body to this immense power of evil and allowed its full force to be absorbed into his body. Returning good for evil, he absorbed the impact of these evil powers and thus neutralized their brunt and broke the back of evil in the world.

Today the floodgates of evil are again threatening to engulf and destroy the human race. A nuclear war could wipe away both the present generation and all future generations. God is looking for victims of love who will offer themselves as a sacrifice to these forces of evil in the same way that Jesus did. We need souls who are willing to make a commitment of love and sacrifice to God for the salvation of our brethren (cf. Isaiah 53). In this very serious period of history, all of us need to take on something of the boldness of the SP. If we follow the example of Jesus, and our Brother St. Francis, we can hope to experience ultimately resurrection and perfect joy.

~ Prayer Suggestion 2 ~

Read Psalm 8

Take a walk through the woods or fields or along the road and look for signs of God's love, beauty, power, wisdom, goodness, balance. Praise and thank God for revealing himself in all the events of history: in one's personal history, in the history of the world, and in the history of salvation. Think of some of the mysteries in God's creation which we cannot understand or explain -for example, the problem of sin and evil in the world. Try to make an act of blind faith and trust in God's wisdom, power, and love even when we cannot see clear manifestations of his wisdom, power, and love.

~ Prayer Suggestion 3 ~

Read Daniel 3:26–90

Spend the remainder of the half hour composing your own canticle of praise of God for all the beauties of His creation. Include the beauties of the inner world of the Spirit, of one's own nature, of friends, as well as of the physical world.

~ Prayer Suggestion 4 ~

Think of the person in the world that you love the most. Ask yourself the following question: How can I see the presence of God in that person? Spend some time praising and thanking God for giving so much goodness, beauty, grace, etc. to that person. Spend some time thanking God for the gift of love whereby you are able to love that person and that person is able to love you.

~ Prayer Suggestion 5 ~

Think of the person that you least like of all your acquaintances. Try to see something of God's goodness, love, life, truth, beauty in that person. What might you do to foster and increase the presence of God in that person? Prayer is always a way to help another.

~ Prayer Suggestion 6 ~

Plan some sort of celebration of gratitude for God's gifts to some particular person or persons you know. It may be a birthday party for a member of your family. It can be something very simple. For example, invite someone for ice cream and cake some afternoon or evening. Make sure that the celebration is centered around praise and gratitude to God for His blessings, His goodness, His love. (Planning and executing this would be a typical Franciscan Prayer in action.)

~ Prayer Suggestion 7 ~

Go outside; look for two trees: one which resembles the kind of person you would like to be or your goal in life, another which expresses in some way the kind of person you see yourself to be now. Decide what you need to do in order to change from the way you now are to the way you would like to be or the way God would like you to be.

~ Prayer Suggestion 8 ~

Praise and thank God for all the good qualities that you find in yourself. How can you more fully develop these good qualities?

~ Prayer Suggestion 9 ~

Watch a beautiful sunset or sunrise. Contemplate the waves of the ocean, a mountain lake, a waterfall, a tree, a leaf, a bee, a beetle, an animal. If you have a telescope, look at one of the planets, especially Saturn or Jupiter. If you have a microscope, study a leaf or a crystal of some sort. As you contemplate God's creation, try to come to a better appreciation of God's beauty, power, goodness, love, wisdom.

~ Prayer Suggestion 10 ~

Plan an act of charity for someone in need; then endeavor to carry it out, either alone or with the help of others.

~ Prayer Suggestion 11 ~

Visit someone sick or old in a nursing home and talk to them about God. Before you leave, pray with this person and ask God to bless and help them. If you do not know anyone ill or aged who lives nearby, simply go unannounced to some nursing home and ask permission to visit some patient who seldom has visitors.

~ Prayer Suggestion 12 ~

Read Ephesians 3:14–21

Write a letter of consolation or condolence to someone who has lost a dear friend in death or who is presently suffering some tragedy in their life. Be sure to talk about God in the letter and close with a prayer, perhaps the passage from Ephesians.

~ Prayer Suggestion 13 ~

If you have available Beethoven's "Ninth Symphony," listen to the Third Movement. (This was the dying request of Pope Pius XII after he had received the last rites of the Church. He wanted to die listening to this very beautiful and peaceful piece of music.) Listen to any other piece of classical, non-vocal music that you find uplifting and spiritual. Other suggestions: Fourth Movement of Beethoven's "Fifth Symphony," "Third Piano Concerto" of Beethoven, "Love Death of Tristan and Isolde" by Wagner.

~ Prayer Suggestion 14 ~

Read slowly Cardinal Newman's poem "Lead Kindly Light" reflecting upon the meaning of each of its phrases. Try to discover a way of applying the words to your own life. (Cardinal Newman wrote these words on the boat coming back from Rome when he was earnestly striving to discover the direction God's light was leading him.) Sing the song several times, and then throughout the rest of the day hum its tune as you go about your duties. Sing it again before retiring.

~ Prayer Suggestion 15 ~

Read aloud Francis Thompson's poem "The Hound of Heaven" or have someone read it aloud to you while you listen. Try to identify with as much of it as you can. How has God pursued your soul like a hound that never gives up? How have you tried to shake off his pursuit of you? What do you need to do now to

surrender yourself completely to Him and His will?
Read once again the pertinent stanzas of the poem.

CHAPTER SEVEN

THOMISTIC PRAYER
& SPIRITUALITY:
THE NT TEMPERAMENT

We have given the name Thomistic to the NT (Intuitive-Thinking) type of prayer, not because it was the only method of prayer recommended by St. Thomas Aquinas, but because it uses the syllogistic method of thinking known as the Scholastic Method which was popularized by Aquinas and his followers. The main emphasis in this type of prayer and spirituality is on the orderly progression of thought from cause to effect. Close attention to the process of rational thinking is required in order to arrive at an appropriate conclusion. Therefore, those persons who have not developed the discipline of logical thinking will usually find this type of prayer very un-prayerlike. They will see it more as study and reflection rather than real prayer. However, if the total method of this prayer, as we suggest it, is used, and the four steps of *Lectio Divina* (Lectio, Meditatio, Oratio, Contemplatio) are followed, all four psychological functions will become involved. Thus, it will be real prayer and not an exclusively intellectual exercise.

Since the time of Descartes, the predominant philosophy of the Western World has been rationalism. These past four centuries have been a field day for the highly intellectual, speculative, rational persons of the NT temperament. Since persons of this temperament, by their very nature, are frequently in positions of leadership in the community, it is easy to understand how this form of prayer came to be recommended above all others in the post-Tridentine period of Church history. Even most of the Jesuit masters of spirituality adapted the Spiritual Exercises to the rationalism of the age. This form of prayer and spirituality was propounded by most Catholic writers from the seventeenth century to the middle of the twentieth century. Most books of meditation written during this period followed the rationalistic approach to prayer.

Indeed, there is a place for this type of prayer, not only for the 10 percent of the population who are of the NT temperament,[1] but also to some extent for all of us. We need a certain amount of exposure to this discursive, reasoning form of prayer. It is highly recommended for use when reflecting upon a virtue or fault and when trying to discover how best to practice the virtue or overcome the fault. It is especially recommended to be used as a method of prayer in preparation for the Sacrament of Penance and Reconciliation.

Characteristics of the NT Temperament

Persons of the NT temperament (which Keirsey identifies with the Greek god Prometheus[2]) possess a very logical mind which approaches a problem with an orderly movement of thought from cause to effect or from effect back to its cause. They gravitate to anything complicated, exacting, or challenging to the mind. NTs have a great thirst for truth and for the freedom that flows from a knowledge of the truth. They have a tremendous desire to understand, comprehend, explain, predict, and thereby control the realities with which they live. The NT wants to master and excel in whatever they attempt, be it sanctity, business, law, administration, etc. They feel compelled to rearrange the environment and are usually leaders in whatever occupation they choose for themselves. The NT tends to be a perfectionist and is alert to their own failures as well as to the shortcomings of others. In the mind of an NT, the worst faults are stupidity and incompetence. The NTs hate to repeat an error. They are even impatient with the initial error; to repeat it becomes anathema. They ruthlessly criticize themselves and others who do not live up to the high standards they have set. Because the NT often has a sense of inadequacy, coupled with a great fear of failure, they are subject to self-doubt and unduly demanding of themselves. NTs tend to be workaholics, scheduling even their play time as they do their work, demanding that they should "have a good time." They must excel even in the games they play, are competitive, and thus apt to be poor losers.

Because Feeling is usually the Inferior Function of the NT, this temperament tends to be impersonal when in relationship with others. Communication with others tends to be terse, precise, logical, with a reluctance to state the obvious. However, they are usually quite straightforward so that one always knows where one stands with them. They are often oblivious to others' emotional responses, insensitive in interpersonal relations, and tend to be unaware of how much their cold impersonal way of acting affects and hurts others. In the presence of a strong NT, others may feel that they do not count. To develop Feeling, which is their Inferior Function, membership and participation in a larger group will help NTs experience the emotional level of the community and by its contagion develop and express their own feelings and emotions. Hence, the great need of NTs for good liturgical celebrations.

Because of their native intelligence and well-developed intuitive abilities, NTs are frequently in positions of leadership. Therefore, their influence on the community is considerably greater than one would assume from the fact that this group is only 10 percent of the general population. NTs delight in planning not only their own life but also the lives of others. Very future-oriented, regarding the past as dead and gone, for the NT what matters most is what might be.

The NT is fascinated by power, not only power over people but power over nature, over ideas, over the future. They have a burning desire to be able to understand, predict, explain, and control every reality. This desire for power is the secret motive behind their intense need for competency and behind the life and actions of many NTs. The desire for competency gives the NT a compulsion to improve and become better than they now are. Because the NT is so serious about learning new knowledge, skills, and competencies, they frequently gain outstanding proficiency in their field of endeavor. What the NT sets out to do, they usually do quite well.

Thomistic Spirituality

The Thomistic approach to spirituality is similar to the approach which the modern physicist or scientist uses in solving a scientific mystery. For example, the NT recognizes it takes much time and effort to investigate the causes behind one's lack of self-discipline and to take the necessary steps to attain the sought virtue. Therefore, an NT will set goals for themselves and will systematically proceed with them. Every fiber of the mind will be challenged to attain the self-discipline to conquer laziness, pride, and selfishness and to center one's life in God and in loving service to others. A logical, step-by-step approach will be the preferred instrument in the NT's total arsenal of spiritual weapons to conquer self-will and submit one's life to the will of God.

The spirituality of the NT temperament will be centered in an earnest pursuit of all the transcendental values: truth, goodness, beauty, unity, love, life, spirit. With their tremendous hunger for perfection, once they have made a choice of God and holiness as their ultimate goal, NTs are willing to exert superhuman effort and energy to attain this goal. An excellent example is St. Teresa of Avila who, from what is known about her life and works, seems to have been an NT; once she chose sanctity, nothing could stop her pursuit of it.

In accord with the NT's desire for competency, the NT temperament seems to have an especial attraction for the higher mansions of spirituality. St. John's NT Gospel has always been the favorite Gospel for mystics and contemplatives. NTs are aware that contemplation is a grace and gift from God but leave no stone unturned in their cooperation with the graces of God that are offered to them. Because of their disdain for second-best, they seek total truth and authenticity in their own life and work hard to reach the whole truth about themselves, about God, about sanctity. This intense search or pursuit of the truth colors their whole spiritual life.

Thomistic Prayer

The type of prayer most suitable to this temperament is the logical, rational, discursive meditation whereby the intellect leads one from one proposition to another until a logical conclusion is drawn in the form of some resolution or ethical demand. All four steps of *Lectio Divina* should be used in Thomistic Prayer; but the main emphasis will be on the orderly progression of thought from cause to effect during the *Meditatio* portion of the prayer. The *Lectio* portion may or may not involve a direct reading of the Bible but may simply begin with some point of revealed teaching of the Bible further developed by theological reflection. Thus, the subject for Thomistic Prayer may be some virtue recommended or some fault condemned by divine revelation.

Thomistic Prayer, which can be referred to as discursive meditation, is not complete when it is confined solely to the rational consideration of a virtue, fault, or religious practice. One needs to respond with feeling and personal involvement to the intellectual consideration and thus involve the heart as well as the head. A person needs to pause and remain still mentally to allow one's Intuitive Function to contribute new insights or inspirations. Thus, all four functions of Sensing, Thinking, Feeling, and Intuition will be activated during Thomistic Prayer. But always the major thrust will be on the role of Thinking and Intuition, since these are the Dominant and Auxiliary Functions of the NT.

In accord with the NT's search for truth, the Thomistic prayer method earnestly seeks to attain the whole truth about the subject chosen for consideration. One looks for new insights from God concerning the virtue to be practiced, the fault to be overcome, the religious practice to be perfected. In this type of prayer, one takes a virtue or fault or theological truth and "walks around it," studying it from every possible angle. To enable one to get a full grasp on the topic chosen for Thomistic Prayer, it is recommended that one uses the seven auxiliary questions – what, why, how, who, where, when, with what helps – and applies each of them to the topic selected. For example, if you used the virtue of faith as the subject for meditation, you would ask the following questions: What do we mean by faith? What is entailed in the practice of faith? What are the reasons to justify the pursuit of faith? Why should I have faith? What is the value of it? How might I practice faith? When and where should it be practiced? Who are some of the people in the Bible and in history who are examples of the practice of faith? Finally, what aids can I use to help me practice faith? The whole exercise concludes with suitable resolutions of how to practice the virtue of faith.

Traditionally, the proponents of this type of prayer recommend that we take some short scriptural phrase or some other appropriate saying as a "spiritual bouquet," which is repeated through the day as a centering or mantra prayer. The purpose of this spiritual nosegay, as it is sometimes called, is to continue the prayerful reflections that begun during the morning meditation.

Unless our discursive reflections during the prayer period result in a change of behavior, they would not be considered authentic Thomistic prayer. Metanoia,[3] or conversion, is an essential element of Thomistic Prayer. A logical step from the new insights into truth received during the meditation is to make the necessary changes in one's life. This would be the practical fruit expected from each exercise of Thomistic Prayer and expressed through one or more resolutions adopted at the conclusion of the discursive meditation.

The Place of Thomistic Prayer Today

Thomistic Prayer and discursive meditation have fallen on hard times in the post-Vatican II church. Part of this is a normal reaction against its over-emphasis during the long post-Tridentine period of history and the Age of Rationalism. When we emphasize one side of a truth too much, the pendulum usually swings to the opposite side of a wholesale rejection of this exaggerated truth. However, we should be very careful lest we lose an important part of our heritage. There is indeed a place for this type of prayer and spirituality, and we all need a certain amount of exposure to this discursive form of prayer. The proper balance will be attained if we use the four steps of *Lectio Divina*. In this way all four functions, Sensing, Thinking, Feeling, and Intuition, will be exercised; and all the temperaments will be able to find some value in it.

Because Thomistic Prayer was often the only form of prayer recommended and taught in seminaries and monasteries, despite how few may have belonged to the NT temperament, we have to wonder how many who were subjected to a steady diet of this type of prayer concluded that they were not among the chosen ones called to sanctity or to the higher mansions of prayer and spirituality. Instead of the guilt engendered because of the many distractions and dryness during the practice of this type of prayer, this should have been seen as the authentic rebellion of one's inner being against the imposition of a wrong form of prayer and spirituality. The mistake was trying to place all beginners in a structured NT-method of prayer. As one progresses in bringing all the functions into conscious, balanced use, the Thinking Function will grasp and utilize this way of praying. (Many of the respondents in the Prayer Project who were clerics, nuns, or religious indicated they were at first quite adverse to this style of prayer; but once into it they were pleasantly surprised by the benefits reaped.)

There is always the danger that this method of prayer becomes an impersonal and objective research or study project and that, although clear thinking is used the emotions and feelings are neglect ed. NTs, and all of us, need to be reminded that, in addition to intellectual conviction, our keen desires must be motivated by love of God. Unless we feel attracted to a teaching because of our love for God and His Will, we will never be motivated to put it into practice. One needs to enter into a prayerful, personal dialogue with God in order to obtain the needed grace and love to carry out our resolutions. Hence, the need of using Oratio and the Feeling Function in Thomistic Prayer.

15 Thomistic-Type Prayer Suggestions

Thomistic Prayer is not meant to be exclusively an intellectual exercise, "a head trip." Besides using our intellect and common sense (practical judgment) to discern exactly what is Christian teaching, we should also use our heart to get in touch with our feelings and emotions. Unless we are attracted to a teaching in the Bible, we will not be motivated to put it into practice. Intellectual conviction indicates the direction our life should take to become Christ-like; but two other elements – God's grace and our love and desire – are essential to pursuing it. To obtain God's grace, a prayerful dialogue with God the Father or Jesus or the Holy

Spirit should be a part of every Thomistic Prayer. Then we must find some way of arousing our feelings of love and desire so that we are willing to put forth the needed psychic energy to carry out our resolutions. In each suggestion of Thomistic Prayer, apply the auxiliary words: what, why, how, when, where, who, with what helps.

~ Prayer Suggestion 1 ~

Read Luke 1:26–38

Consider and contemplate the faith of Mary, who is a great saint primarily because of her faith. Faith means the total commitment and blind trust of our lives into the hands of God. We can understand the meaning of faith by seeing it exemplified in the life of another person. Write down the qualities of Mary's faith as you see them exemplified in the Annunciation. What changes do you need to make in your life in order to bring your faith more into conformity with Mary's faith?

~ Prayer Suggestion 2 ~

Read Luke 1:39–46

Consider the ministry of Mary toward her cousin Elizabeth. Without any thought of herself, Mary unselfishly hurried to the aid of an old woman having her first baby and remained there until after the birth of John. Mary may be seen as the first "Eucharistic Minister" bringing the flesh and blood of Jesus to the home of Elizabeth and Zachary. What might we do to minister better to the needs of others?

~ Prayer Suggestion 3 ~

Read Mark 9:33–37

Spiritual Childhood: virtues of simplicity, trust, charity, purity of intention. What does Jesus mean when he says that we must become as little children if we wish to enter the Kingdom of Heaven? What are the qualities of a small child that are especially needed in our relationship with God? Which of these qualities do you need to intensify and develop at the present time in your life? (See *The Autobiography of St. Thérèse.*[4])

~ Prayer Suggestion 4 ~

Read Mark 8:34–38

Doctrine of the Cross: What does Jesus mean when he insists that in order to be his disciple we must take up our cross and follow him? What are the crosses in your present life? Are you carrying them in the same way that Jesus carried his cross to Calvary? What do you need to change in your present attitude toward your crosses?

~ Prayer Suggestion 5 ~

Read Matthew 10:39

"He who seeks only himself brings himself to ruin; whereas he who brings himself to naught for my sake discovers who he really is." What does Jesus mean by the words "bring oneself to naught for my sake"? What do you need to do in your life to put Jesus's concerns ahead of your own? How does self-discipline enable us to "discover who we really are"? Just who are we really? What is our primary purpose on earth? Is it to satisfy ourselves or to fulfill some God-given destiny? What is the ministry God is asking of us?

~ Prayer Suggestion 6 ~

Read Matthew 5:20–26 and John 2:13-17

What is the difference between the anger of Jesus and the anger which Jesus condemns in this passage from Matthew? Why is anger so wrong that Jesus equates it with the command against killing? St. Thomas defines anger as the desire to attack violently anyone who poses a threat to something we consider valuable. What about self-defense of our country, our family, ourselves? How far are we justified to go to defend ourselves? Is the anger you sometimes feel a justifiable anger, similar to that of Jesus, or the kind of anger Jesus condemns in the Sermon on the Mount? What does one do about one's anger?

~ Prayer Suggestion 7 ~

Read Matthew 6:26–34

Study carefully each verse of Jesus's teaching about Divine Providence. With what of it do you agree? What do you consider not applicable to your present way of life? What justification can you make for the verses you are unwilling to accept literally? What changes do you need to make in your life in order to follow Christ's teachings here?

~ Prayer Suggestion 8 ~

Read Matthew 6:19–25

How does this teaching of Jesus differ from the generally accepted practice and teaching of today's world? How far are you willing to go to follow Jesus in his teaching about true riches? In what ways are you trying to serve two masters? In your life who are the different masters determining what you do; how you act; where you spend your time, money, energy? What practical changes do you need to make in your present life in order to bring it more into accord with the teaching of Jesus?

~ Prayer Suggestion 9 ~

Read Matthew 5:23–24

"If you bring your gift to the altar and there recall that your brother has anything against you, leave you r gift at the altar, and go first to be reconciled with your brother, then come and offer your gift." Are you willing to take this command of Jesus literally? Do you believe that it is more important to be reconciled with others than it is to go to Mass on Sunday? At present is there anyone in your life who is not reconciled with you? Have you tried to become reconciled with them?

Have you tried as much as you should? As much as God would want you to do? Do you really love that person who is not reconciled to you? What more can you do to become reconciled with those who have something against you? Even if the "thing against you" is not real (i.e., imaginary), is there anything you should do to bring about an understanding between the two of you?

~ Prayer Suggestion 10 ~

Read Matthew 13:44–46

"The Kingdom of God is like a treasure hidden in a field, which a man finds and rejoicing goes and sells all he has in order to buy the field." Where have you discovered the hidden treasure of the Kingdom of God? Are you willing to sell everything in order to possess it? Have you disposed of everything else in order to obtain it? Do you sufficiently appreciate the hidden treasure of God 's Kingdom? What do you need to do to appreciate better this "hidden treasure," "this pearl of great price"?

~ Prayer Suggestion 11~

Read Mark 10:35–45

Read the passage carefully. Notice that Jesus in no way condemns ambition but simply teaches the disciples that their desire to be first should be in the area of humble service to others. "Whoever wants to rank first among you must serve the needs of all." Do you have this kind of ambition? What do you need to change in your present way of life in order to do a better job of serving others? How might you, like Jesus, give your life in ransom for others?

~ Prayer Suggestion 12 ~

Read Matthew 11:29; Luke 14:7–11; I Corinthians 4:7

Take the virtue of humility (or choose another virtue). Reflect upon it. What does it mean? What is the connection between humility and authenticity? What does Jesus mean when he says, "Learn of me because I am meek and humble of heart." If you have some good spiritual book, you might read what it says about the virtue of humility. Think of some examples of persons in the Bible who were humble (Moses, Mary, Joseph). Where have you been humble in the past? What are some examples of your failure to be humble? What changes do you need to make in your life in order to be humbler? What do you need to do in order to grow in humility? What might you do this day to practice humility? End the period of prayer with petitions to God, Jesus, Mary, and the saints to help you to be humbler.

~ Prayer Suggestion 13 ~

Read Mark 15:10; Acts 13:48

Consider the fault of envy (or choose another fault). Reflect upon its meaning. St. Thomas defines envy as the evil sadness one feels at the success of a rival or peer. Have you ever felt envy? When? Why? What did you do about it? Have you ever suffered as a result of the envy of someone else? What did you do about it? How was envy the cause of the death of Jesus? Why do people experience envy? Why are envious people often unaware of their envy? How might you discover whether you still harbor secret envy toward others? What might you do to avoid being envious of others? How is love the opposite of envy? End the period of prayer with fervent petitions to God asking Him to help you discover your secret envy and to help you overcome it.

~ Prayer Suggestion 14 ~

Read Philippians 2:4–8

"Your attitude must be that of Christ." What does St. Paul say is the attitude of Christ? (We must empty ourselves.) What is there within me that needs to be emptied? St. Paul says that we must take the form of a servant or slave. What exactly does this entail in my attitude toward those with whom I live, work, associate? What changes do I need to make in my life in order to bring it more into conformity with that of Jesus? What steps do I need to take to bring about a more Christ-like attitude toward myself, toward others, toward God? End the period of prayer with fervent petitions to God for the grace to carry out whatever resolutions your conscience has revealed during the reflections upon this text of Philippians.

~ Prayer Suggestion 15 ~

Read James 2:14–26

Virtue of Charity: What efforts am I making to serve the poor, the suffering, the needy people of my community? What am I doing for the poor and needy and suffering people of the world? Do I really believe that they are my brothers and sisters? What in the area of charity can I do to fulfill Christ's command to love others as He has loved us? "Faith without works is as dead as a body without breath."

CHAPTER EIGHT

USING OUR SHADOW
& INFERIOR FUNCTION
IN PRAYER

Carl Jung described the Shadow as the unconscious half of our human nature. When most people think of their shadow, they think of it as something primitive and evil, something to be avoided and hidden, rather than brought to the light of prayer. But Jung was of the opinion that 80 percent of the shadow is gold ore waiting to be dug out of the depths of our unconscious and put to work in our conscious lives. This unconscious side of the human psyche, which is the source of all that is best as well as all that is worst in an individual or society, contains both primitive, undeveloped, inferior qualities and an unlimited, unrealized potential for good. The shadow is psychic energy within our soul waiting to be brought into consciousness and put to good use in the service of God, our fellow human beings, and ourselves.

The Myers-Briggs Type Indicator measures our relationship with the outer world and our actions and reactions as we respond to it. During the first 30 years of life, one's focus is typically on strengthening the preferred attitudes and functions of the one's type. However, following the laws of complementarity, the opposite of our MBTI score should give us our hidden, inner temperament, which is an integral part of our shadow. During the second half of life, one should begin to deal seriously with one's shadow, including the shadow side of the MBTI.

A good way to begin the process of using one's shadow in prayer is to read the portrait of the temperament and type that is directly opposite one's MBTI score. For example, if one's type is INFP, then one's MBTI shadow will be ESTJ (see the characteristics as described by Myers and Briggs or by Keirsey and Bates[1]). One can presume that the things described in this opposite temperament and type are part of the qualities of one's positive shadow which have remained somewhat undeveloped and unconscious.

In the second half of life, one should attempt to activate these qualities of the shadow and bring them into some sort of balance with the qualities of one's conscious life which were developed earlier. The shadow becomes negative and evil only when that part of it, which Divine Providence wills to become conscious, is repressed and denied conscious expression. God gives us sufficient psychic energy each day to handle that part of the shadow which is ready to be gathered into consciousness and put to good use. The daily, formal period of prayer and meditation is a perfect time to connect with that part of the shadow which is ripe for harvesting.[2]

The Role of the MBTI Functions in Prayer

One of the many marvels of creation is that, in endowing human nature with the four psychological functions of Sensation, Intuition, Thinking and Feeling, God created humans in such a way that they are capable of perceiving and operating at the level of physical reality as well as at the numinous[3] level of the spirit. Each of the four functions is like a swinging door which can swing out to relate to the external world of physical reality and inward to relate to the inner world of the spirit. However, the four functions operate differently when relating to the transcendental level of reality than when relating to the obvious physical world.

Just as is the case with developing the shadow side of one's MBTI score, so too may working with the less preferred and well-developed MBTI Functions be an excellent way to enhance one's prayer life and relationship with God and others. In order to pave the way for this endeavor, an understanding of the following information will be useful.

While there are four sets of preferences in the MBTI – E/I, S/N, T/F, and J/P – only four are termed psychological functions: Thinking, Feeling, Sensing, and Intuition.[4]

In addition, the ability to make use of these functions can be characterized as Dominant, indicating greater ability; Auxiliary, or helper, which indicates less ability and is usually in support of the Dominant function; Tertiary, which is even less subject to control; and Inferior, the function most difficult to access and control. Moreover, in a given individual, the functions can be classified as conscious or unconscious, and either extraverted or introverted.

The classification of each function – its ranking as to dominant, auxiliary, tertiary or inferior; whether it is extraverted or introverted or conscious or unconscious – varies according to one's particular MBTI type. While this may seem complicated, once you know your MBTI type, the way your four functions are categorized and their particular characteristics, the discussion of what follows, and why it is of value in terms of your prayer life, will be understandable.

Classifying the Four Functions According to Relative Dominance

- The dominant function is determined by whether one prefers the attitude of judging (J) or perceiving (P), and whether one is extraverted or introverted.
  - o If one is Extraverted (E) and Judging (J), Thinking (T) or Feeling (F) will be the primary function. If one is extraverted and Perceiving (P), Sensing (S) or Intuition (N) will be the primary function.
  - o If one is Introverted (I) and Judging (J), Sensing (S) or Intuition (N) will be the primary function. If one is introverted and Perceiving (P), Thinking (T) or Feeling (F) will be the primary function.
- The auxiliary function reverses the script. For those whose dominant function is T or F, the preferred perceiving function (S or N) will be the auxiliary. For those whose dominant function is S or N, the preferred judging function (T or F) will be the auxiliary.
- The tertiary function will be the opposite of the auxiliary function, and the inferior function will be the opposite of the dominant function.

Classifying the Four Functions According to Extraversion and Introversion

- Starting with the dominant function, it will be extraverted for extraverts and introverted for introverts.
- The auxiliary function will be the opposite of the dominant function. If the dominant function is

extraverted, the auxiliary function will be introverted. If the dominant function is introverted, the auxiliary function will be extraverted.

- The tertiary function will be the same as the primary function: for introverts, the dominant and tertiary functions will be introverted; while for extraverts, the dominant and tertiary functions will be extraverted.[5]

- The inferior function will always be the opposite of the primary function.

Chart 1: Relative Dominance and Extraverted (E) and Introverted (I) Functions of the Sixteen MBTI Types

ENFJ	Dominant-Feeling (E) Auxiliary-Intuition (I)	Inferior (4th)-Thinking (I) Tertiary (3rd)-Sensing (E)
ENFP	Dominant-Intuition (E) Auxiliary-Feeling (I)	Inferior (4th)-Sensing (I) Tertiary (3rd)-Thinking (E)
INFJ	Dominant-Intuition (I) Auxiliary-Feeling (E)	Inferior (4th)-Sensing (E) Tertiary (3rd)-Thinking (I)
INFP	Dominant-Feeling (I) Auxiliary-Intuition (E)	Inferior (4th)-Thinking (E) Tertiary (3rd)-Sensing (I)
ESFJ	Dominant-Feeling (E) Auxiliary-Sensing (I)	Inferior (4th)-Thinking (I) Tertiary (3rd)-Intuition (E)
ISFJ	Dominant-Sensing (I) Auxiliary-Feeling (E)	Inferior (4th)-Intuition (E) Tertiary (3rd)-Thinking (I)
ESFP	Dominant-Sensing (E) Auxiliary-Feeling (I)	Inferior (4th)-Intuition (I) Tertiary (3rd)-Thinking (E)
ISFP	Dominant-Feeling (I) Auxiliary-Sensing (E)	Inferior (4th)-Thinking (E) Tertiary (3rd)-Intuition (I)
ESTJ	Dominant-Thinking (E) Auxiliary-Sensing (I)	Inferior (4th)-Feeling (I) Tertiary (3rd)-Intuition (E)
ISTJ	Dominant-Sensing (I) Auxiliary-Thinking (E)	Inferior (4th)-Intuition (E) Tertiary (3rd)-Feeling (I)

ESTP	Dominant-Sensing (E) Auxiliary-Thinking (I)	Inferior (4th)-Intuition (I) Tertiary (3rd)-Feeling (E)
ISTP	Dominant-Thinking (I) Auxiliary-Sensing (E)	Inferior (4th)-Feeling (E) Tertiary (3rd)-Intuition (I)
ENTJ	Dominant-Thinking (E) Auxiliary-Intuition (I)	Inferior (4th)-Feeling (I) Tertiary (3rd)-Sensing (E)
ENTP	Dominant-Intuition (E) Auxiliary-Thinking (I)	Inferior (4th)-Sensing (I) Tertiary (3rd)-Feeling (E)
INTJ	Dominant-Intuition (I) Auxiliary-Thinking (E)	Inferior (4th)-Sensing (E) Tertiary (3rd)-Feeling (E)
INTP	Dominant-Thinking (I) Auxiliary-Intuition (E)	Inferior (4th)-Feeling (E) Tertiary (3rd)-Sensing (I)

The Transcendent Dimension of the Inferior Function

In his writings, Jung frequently talks about the transcendent function of the human psyche. By this he meant the tendency of the four psychological functions to be both conscious and unconscious, thus unifying physical realities with the inner, spiritual realm. Therefore, each of the functions can be said to have a transcendent dimension. One of the characteristics of the transcendent dimension is its ability to bring together seemingly irreconcilable opposites in the form of a symbol.[6] The classic religious example is the cross, which reconciles life and death by means of resurrection.

The symbols generated by the transcendent dimension arise from the unconscious, most often during prayer and in the form of dreams and visions. Operating this way, the transcendent dimension of the functions allows us to connect with the metaphysical, spiritual levels of reality, including God, the soul, truth, goodness, beauty, unity, freedom, love, etc., shedding illumination on them through the unifying symbols described above, so that they are incorporated into our consciousness.

During prayer, we seek to activate the transcendent dimension of each of the four functions, since there is much grace and unconscious psychic energy at each of these four doorways to the inner world of the spirit. Special consideration should be given to the activation of the transcendent dimension of the Inferior and Tertiary functions (the functions with which we have the least proficiency) since, according to Jung, most of the undifferentiated psychic energy lies concealed behind these two doorways in the unconscious, spiritual areas of life. It is here we will find our shadow.

The Swiss Jungian psychologist and scholar Marie-Louise von Franz states: "The inferior function holds the secret key to the unconscious totality of the person."[7] Therefore, if we wish to attain wholeness, maturity, sanctity, we need to work especially with our Inferior and Tertiary Functions. Because they are hidden in the deeper realms of the shadow, we frequently neglect to develop them. We reach wholeness only when we are willing to engage in the effort and discipline necessary to bring about a working relationship between the Ego (the focal point of our conscious life),[8] the shadow (the unconscious depths of our inner self), and God. Only when a good partnership between these three is established will we reach the destiny for which we were created. One purpose of daily prayer and meditation is to attain this working relationship.

The Inferior Function always has a mysterious quality because of its unconscious contents. While being the weakest spot in the armor of our conscious life, it is nevertheless the depository of great unconscious potential; but until this potential is brought to the surface of consciousness, it remains undifferentiated, i.e., able to go either in the direction of good or in the direction of evil. When the Inferior Function is denied or rejected, we get along tolerably well until some unexpected eruption of the shadow overtakes us. Then we can expect trouble because, when neglected, the Inferior Function tends to become negative and teams up with the evil elements of the shadow.

By becoming consciously aware of our Inferior Function, we can undertake its transformation and reduce its compulsive eruption and awkwardness. During the second half of life, after we have somewhat mastered the use of our Dominant and Auxiliary Functions, we can expect frequent manifestations of the emerging Inferior Function. If we develop its potential, we will create a whole new world of possibilities and a whole new outlook on life for ourselves. When the Inferior Function is allowed to operate without our conscious control, it is like opening a Pandora's box. The contents of the unconscious spill out helter-skelter. On the other hand, if we repress or deny the Inferior Function, we keep the door closed to the riches lying buried in the unconscious. By acknowledging our inferior qualities, we open ourselves to pain, suffering, struggle, and conflict; but the incorporation of our Inferior Function into consciousness will lead to the wholeness and balance which is the mark of a mature person.

Generally, we are very touchy and easily hurt when the deficiencies of our Inferior Function are pointed out to us. In this area, whether it is Sensing, Intuition, Thinking, or Feeling, we are the most uncertain of ourselves. We have no tight rein of conscious control over the Inferior Function as we do over our Dominant and Auxiliary Functions, and so the Inferior Function will often express itself in highly emotional, erratic, or infantile behavior. It comes and goes as it likes and marches to an unconscious drummer. When used, the Inferior Function is generally slow, cumbersome, unadapted and requires a great outlay of psychic energy which quickly exhausts us. Frequently we find ourselves crucified between the Inferior Function and the Dominant Function, which often tries to thwart and by-pass our weaker functions by playing to our egocentricity. The Inferior Function is our greatest problem and our greatest challenge.

Everything in the unconscious earnestly seeks and desires to become conscious. However, in the plan of God there is a proper order and time for each element of the unconscious to become conscious. If we would open at once all four doorways of Sensing, Intuition, Thinking and Feeling to the unconscious, our conscious life would soon be flooded out or overwhelmed. This condition is called a psychosis. These doors must be opened gradually, one by one, and entered. The hour set aside for prayer or meditation is the ideal time to connect with the inner, spiritual, unconscious areas of life. Prayer, then, can include the active use of our unconscious faculties to foster the proper and easy entrance of the psychic energies from the unconscious shadow into our ordinary life and activities. A more traditional way of saying the same thing would be to say that prayer is the exercise which puts us in contact with the Spirit of God dwelling within our inner being.

Even those in the higher mansions of contemplative prayer must use their conscious faculties[9] during prayer to connect with the Holy Spirit. Non-believers in God, even if they may call it meditation or some other word, must also rely upon what we call prayer to contact their inner psyche. The activation of the transcendent dimension of all four functions will enable us to connect with the psychic powers and energies of God and spirit. Using the Inferior and Tertiary Functions during the time we set aside for prayer and meditation will give us some of our most valuable faith experiences because a new dimension of practice will allow us to see God and inner realities in a different way. To a similar but somewhat lesser extent, everything we have said about the Inferior Function can also be said about the Tertiary Function.

Activating the Transcendent Dimension of the Sensing Function

The transcendent dimension of the Sensation Function is activated by one's sensible imagination; and, if properly used, both Franciscan and Ignatian Prayer methods will accomplish this. By using active imagination,[10] we open the doorway to our shadow and allow some reconciling symbol to appear. In a flash, this symbol may reveal a new dimension of God or a new insight into one of the facets of our faith or of our relationship with God. Through sensible images, comparisons, analogies, and parables we are led to a better understanding of the mysteries of God.

For example, contemplation of the beauties and powers of nature may open the doorway to some symbol or insight that will help us understand a mystery of God. An example of a memorable experience of this can be had on a visit to the Niagara Falls. Standing at the bottom of the Falls, close to the powerful waves of water sweeping over and down, one appreciates more fully the infinite power of God. The thought comes: "All of this mighty power I am seeing and hearing here is only a drop in the ocean compared to the power of God." The time at the bottom of the falls becomes a beautiful and powerful experience of faith-filled awe and prayer that stays with one for many days thereafter.

Something similar can happen when one watches a sunset or sunrise. A sunrise is a daily symbol of birth and new life, while each sunset can be a symbol of death. If one is attuned to the grace of God while observing these phenomena of nature, one understands a little better one's relationship to life and death and the promise of resurrection. The amazing thing is that one can watch a thousand sunrises and sunsets and each time the symbolism of life and death becomes more alive and meaningful.

A new understanding of God and the transcendentals also occurs when one listens to a beautiful piece of music, or watches the ocean waves, or contemplates a snow-covered mountain. Modern photography, especially slow motion, easily activates the transcendent dimension of Sensing. With some effort, we can activate the transcendent dimension of all five of our senses: seeing, hearing, touching, tasting, smelling; and thus, the Sensing Function becomes the doorway through which a spiritual insight into the inner world becomes consciously present.

Interestingly enough, people whose Tertiary or Inferior Function is Sensing usually have an easier time activating the transcendent dimension of this function. When Sensing is the Dominant or Auxiliary Function, one tends to get lost in the welter of sensible details and sense impressions that bombard one. Whereas, when Sensing is the Inferior or Tertiary Function, the tendency is to cut through and ignore extraneous details, and go to the very heart of the reality. Instead of being distracted by too many details, one quickly and easily sees the inner beauty, power, order, harmony, wholeness of God shining through His creation. Whether contemplating the macrocosm of the physical universe or the microcosm of a single cell this will be true. With some special effort, however, those whose Dominant or Auxiliary Function is Sensing can learn to activate its transcendent dimension and use it well during prayer. A Sensing person, who will do a rote action, for example, saying a rosary, listening to a waterfall, dabbing paint on a canvas or other object, will find that this continuous, almost rhythmic, sense-overload will often trigger one's active imagination into a contemplation of the mysteries of God or one of the transcendental values.

Activating the Transcendent Dimension of the Intuitive Function

Of the four functions, the transcendent dimension of Intuition is probably the easiest to activate in order to get in touch with the inner world and the transcendent realities of God and spirit. Since the basic purpose of Intuition is to catch the symbols that rise from the unconscious, to use it during prayer may be comparatively easy; but if this is the Dominant or Auxiliary Function, one must develop the ability to cut through the many extraneous symbols and recognize the really important ones.

Intuition apprehends those symbols or images which tie together opposite poles of truth. Intuition discovers the synthesis that maintains the balance between thesis and antithesis. This in turn is productive of new energy and grace. By using one's creative imagination, a balance is established between the conscious and unconscious, between the physical and spiritual, between God and creation, between nature and grace.

The transcendent dimension of Intuition opens the veil hiding the future from us, enabling us to read the signs of the time and discern the future directions and the future possibilities of our life. Time, leisure, and patient waiting will allow the creative imagination to produce the inspiration that gives new insights into God and our relationship to God. Intuition enables us to discern God's will for ourselves and others for both the immediate and distant future, to see God's providence and loving care, and to experience the untapped potential for good that has not yet been actualized in ourselves and in the community.

Because of the modern prejudice in favor of the physical and rational and against the spiritual and metaphysical, those who have Intuition as a Tertiary or Inferior Function may be wary and afraid of it and thus find it difficult to activate its transcendent dimension. The important thing is to give due consideration to any sudden insights that seek one's attention. If they are neglected and not taken seriously, they become lost in the welter of sensible images which fill our daily life. These inspirations need to be caught on the fly since they quickly come and go. If we fail to take hold of them when they are fleetingly presented, they pass by and are lost. To retain them it is advisable to write them down as soon as they appear.

One of the best ways to begin to use or develop the transcendent dimension of Intuition is to pay attention to one's dreams. Dreams are the voice of the unconscious which reveals itself to us every night. Dream language is always the language of symbols, and we need our Intuitive Function to discern their meaning. Dreams should be regularly and conscientiously jotted down in a notebook which is kept ready at the side of one's bed. They should then be taken to prayer and reflected upon to discover any insight which will enable us to understand better one or the other of the transcendental values and thus deepen our relationship with God and our inner self.

Those who do not remember their dreams can use other methods to activate the creative imagination during waking hours including Initiated Symbol Projection (ISP).[11] Since symbols are a visible expression of something invisible, they are a way that we may get in touch with the depths and heights of our spiritual potential, or we can see them as something that God, the Holy Spirit, is trying to communicate with us. You could say that ISP is another form of prayer, another way of relating to God and to the spiritual, transcendental dimensions of reality.

The Augustinian method of prayer is the best type of prayer to activate the transcendent dimension of Intuition. The emphasis here is on discovery of some symbol or insight that makes a spiritual truth more real in our life. We may come to understand how to reconcile two opposite truths or values – for example, justice and mercy, truth and compassion for the sinner, gentleness and severity, confrontation and non-violence, etc. We should also reflect upon the symbols used in our Christian religious practices, especially in the liturgy, e. g., the Incarnation which unites God and human nature or the Paschal Mystery which ties together death and resurrection. Through the use of the transcendent dimension of Intuition we will find new meaning in these expressions of our faith.

Activating the Transcendent Dimension of the Thinking Function

Through the transcendent dimension of the Thinking Function, we come to a deeper understanding of God's truth and justice in relationship to us and in our relationship to God. When Thinking is operating at a transcendent level, it grasps the unifying symbol which ties together apparently contradictory and opposing truths. One is enabled to simplify complex issues and make them understandable to others in simple terms. Thinking works both at the conscious level and the unconscious level, but it cannot work simultaneously at full force at both levels. We must slow down the conscious level of thinking and give the mind the needed leisure to allow the unconscious, transcendent dimension of Thinking to operate. Once this happens, we will be surprised at the sudden creative insights that allow us to see a common denominator which brings together a whole series of disparate facts or truths.

When Thinking is the Inferior Function, it can have a powerful influence during prayer when its transcendent dimension is activated. Rather than becoming lost in a labyrinth of individual truths, a unifying symbol or truth brings many truths together. In other words, we are able to simplify a complex issue containing diverse truths and perceive something that unites them and bridges the differences between them. In turn, this unifying symbol becomes a new experience of truth which brings delight to the one receiving it and clarification and enlightenment to others. A synthesis of the total is obtained without all the extraneous facts and details. A person with a Dominant Thinking Function may denigrate this but will have to admit that, simplistic as it may seem, a plausible but logical conclusion has been reached nevertheless.

The Thomistic type of prayer can be used to activate the transcendent dimension of the Thinking Function. The purpose of Thomistic Prayer is to delve deeply into revealed truths and allow recognition of the reconciling or unifying symbol that will bring together the apparently opposite poles of truth. Reading and studying Scripture themes, reflecting on doctrine or ethics, considering one's attitude in an examination of conscience are ways of activating the transcendent dimension of the Thinking Function. For example, one might consider the problem of how and why an all-powerful, allloving, all-good, all-wise God allows so much evil in the world and our own part in it. If we succeed in activating the transcendent dimension of Thinking, we may receive an insight into these apparently contradictory realities. This sudden enlightenment into the truth brings joy, freedom, and peace. "You shall know the truth and the truth shall make you free" (John 8:32). Because Thomistic Prayer makes use of both Thinking and Intuition, it is a most valuable source of new insights into the truths of God, the world, and our religion.

Activating the Transcendent Dimension of the Feeling Function

The transcendent dimension of the Feeling Function helps one to experience the transcendental values of goodness, love, and mercy in a personal way and not as a mere impersonal tenet of belief. The Feeling Function penetrates external appearances and acknowledges the value and worth of the inner person, be it God, Jesus, or another human being. Rationalists, tyrants, and oppressors, who treat others as chattel or objects to be bought, sold, and used as one would an animal or inanimate object, ignore this dimension of personhood. But, once we have grasped this personal dimension of another, we will respect the other's freedom, dignity, and independence.

Through the transcendent dimension of Feeling we make God, Jesus, and the Holy Spirit living persons, who are just as real as the human beings with whom we associate. This in turn enables us to experience the giving and receiving of love between God and ourselves. When Feeling is the Dominant Function, the problem with its use in prayer is that one is overwhelmed with a host of different feelings. Whereas, when the Feeling Function is the Inferior or Tertiary Function, it is often easier to filter out what is really important and apply it to one's relationship with God without being drowned in a sea of confusing emotions. When we activate the transcendent dimension of the Feeling Function, we know instinctively the direction into which God's will is calling us and respond accordingly either by gentleness or severity, tolerance or confrontation, justice or mercy.

At the conscious level Feeling operates through love, joy, peace, patience, gentleness, generosity. At the unconscious level the Feeling Function picks up the mood and feelings of an individual or group and the vibrations of the unconscious, spiritual powers, including God. Therefore, those who have repressed or neglected to use their Feeling Function will be helped in the activation of their feelings at a transcendental level by participating in large or small assemblies such as prayer or faith sharing groups. For example, a good experience of communal liturgy will enable them to release their Feeling Function.

Three methods of prayer – Augustinian, Franciscan, and Ignatian – can activate the transcendent dimension of the Feeling Function. Thomistic Prayer also may be used if care is taken to add the recommended *Oratio* and *Contemplatio*, the colloquies and aspirations. One might say that activating the transcendent dimension of the Feeling Function is the basic goal of all prayer, since the purpose of prayer is to establish a personal relationship with God, Jesus, and the Holy Spirit. This is what religion and prayer are all about - to bring us to an experience of a union of love with the person of God. If we open ourselves to the graces of the Spirit of the Lord, realizing and working with the four psychological functions and attitudes will bring forth a whole new dimension of relationship, knowledge, and understanding not only of ourselves and others but also of the transcendental values and God.

141

Extraverted and Introverted Functions

In addition to the realization that we have a dominant and auxiliary, and some lesser adept functions, an important help to developing and utilizing the four functions in prayer and spirituality is to understand the by-play of the extraversion and introversion of these functions. As explained in Chapter Nine, it seems furthermore that all four functions have a transcendent dimension which enables us to have experiences of contact with God. Experience shows that the introverted functions are easiest to use in prayer, while the extraverted functions are more suitable for our relationships with other human beings and in our activities in the external world, i.e., our lifestyle or spirituality. Therefore, it follows that the transcendent dimension of our introverted functions is usually the easiest to activate and use during prayer.

During prayer, extraverts will use their introverted auxiliary function primarily since this will be the easiest way for them to activate the transcendent dimension. Since one's conscious will ordinarily lacks direct control over the inferior function, it is not recommended that extraverts attempt to activate its transcendent dimension in their normal, daily prayer period. However, when an extravert has learned the secret of how one's least preferred function behaves or comports itself, if this inferior function is activated either during prayer or just in repose, one can expect some very powerful, deep, and lasting faith experiences of God's presence, power, and love. We must not forget, however, that all of us are capable of using all four functions in prayer. It simply takes more psychic energy to activate the tertiary and fourth (inferior) functions. Because all of us are somewhat lazy, or perhaps over-extended, or not too knowledgeable about our inferior function, we have the tendency to use the dominant and auxiliary functions primarily. This results in our particular personality type.

For introverts, the dominant and tertiary functions will be the two best functions to use during prayer since both of them are introverted. Our observation is that introverts will frequently have the most powerful experiences of God during prayer when they succeed in activating the transcendent dimension of their tertiary function. Although the dominant function of the introvert is introverted, it is still the function used in external activities even though its use is hidden to the outside observer. However, unless the introvert has developed a very high degree of self-discipline, they will experience many worldly distractions when using the dominant function in prayer.

Furthermore, the introvert will usually have more success in prayer by using the introverted tertiary function than by trying to activate the transcendent dimension of the extraverted auxiliary function, the function shown to the world. However, the auxiliary and tertiary functions work similar to a seesaw, so that when one is consciously activated, the other one regresses into the unconscious area of our psyche. Therefore, for the introvert the tertiary function can usually be controlled during the prayer period by the conscious will. Since it is naturally introverted, it is the easiest function to use when connecting with God during prayer.

Using the Extraverted Third or Fourth Function

Once an introvert sufficiently matures to discover how to activate the fourth, or least used extraverted function, the employment of this function may make the greatest impact on the world and others. On the other hand, for the extravert, since the inferior function will always be introverted, the extraverted tertiary function will probably have the most impact on others. Just as the two introverted functions are best suited for communing with God, so also the two extraverted functions will be the ones whereby we will have our greatest influence on other people and the world in which we live.

After we are dead and gone, the probability is that our most lasting influence on the world, either for good or evil, will be those things accomplished by the activation of our extraverted third or fourth function. These functions are most deeply buried in our unconscious and are closest to our inner Self, the center of our being. They are most powerful and most open to the operations of the Holy Spirit in our life. Moreover, their activation usually takes place later in life when many ego demands have been settled. Differentiation of these functions, along with one's already differentiated dominant and auxiliary, allows one to proceed with more wisdom and understanding, with more surety and serenity. Therefore, it behooves us to work to discover and to use whatever means needed to develop our tertiary and inferior functions. Learning to use the third and fourth function in prayer is an excellent method for activating and developing our ability to use these functions in other areas of our life.

One, however, is advised not to try too early in life to activate the fourth function. There seems to be an order that needs to be observed if there is to be a balanced and healthy use of all four functions. One learns first how to use one's dominant function in a balanced, disciplined, unselfish, mature way. The hope is that we might have attained this by the age of 25 or 30. Next comes the maturation of our auxiliary function, followed by an actualization and disciplined use of our tertiary function. Only after we have reasonable control of the first three functions should we make a serious conscious attempt to develop a balanced use of the fourth or inferior function.

No matter how old or mature we may be, we must never forget that the fourth function marches to a different drummer. We seem to be able to control the first three functions more or less directly by our conscious will, provided we have learned the art of good self-discipline. The fourth function does not seem to be subject directly to our conscious will. It seems to obey only the secret voice of our inner Self, a deeper authority than our ego-controlled will.

As we become more mature and self-disciplined, the inner Self is able to take fuller possession of our life and actions. When this occurs we gradually learn how to activate and use the fourth function. Leisure, play, relaxation, freedom from stress, and plenty of rest are some of the ways which bring forth our fourth function to be used to the best advantage. Prayer and meditation, openness to God and God's will, are other ways to encourage our fourth function to become active in our life. We need to empty ourselves of our power drive, our ambition to control our own lives, and surrender ourselves to a higher power, that of God and the Holy Spirit. We need to practice detachment from external pressures to be thus or so, which is the dying to ourselves which Jesus recommends in the Gospel (see Matthew 10:39).

Thinking as the Fourth Function

There are many examples of how the activation of the transcendent dimension of the extraverted third or fourth function produces good, long-lasting effects upon society. If this function is thinking, its transcendent dimension enables one to simplify complex and involved thinking processes. Once one finds the right combination of leisure and work that unlocks the power of the extraverted, but not dominant, thinking function, one is able to take the complex and involved ideas of others and express them in simple, straight-forward words easily understood by ordinary people of limited education.

This ability to give a clear, compact summary of complicated thoughts will prove to be of great value to others. In this way, persons whose third or fourth function is thinking can make a lasting imprint on their environment.

Feeling as the Fourth Function

If feeling is one's inferior or fourth function, the simplicity of the valuing process will allow one to appreciate the values, differences and commonality of others. If one has matured sufficiently to activate the inferior function of feeling, one can become a good peace-maker in today's violent and alienated world. Such a person may succeed in reconciling not only alienated individuals but also whole nations and races.

We may speculate that Mohandas K. Gandhi and Martin Luther King, Jr. were ENTJ or INTP, with thinking as their dominant function and feeling as their inferior function. Like a typical NT, Gandhi emphasized in his teachings and actions the all-importance of truth – *Satyagraha*. He chose the typical NT profession of law and became an excellent trial lawyer. Yet, in reading his biography one is struck by his inferior feeling function in his relationships with his wife and family. Similarly, the early life of King was a pursuit of truth and higher education, yet his incarceration in the Birmingham jail seems to have triggered his feeling function.[12] Both Gandhi and King activated their feeling function through self-discipline, suffering, and growth in maturity and thus were able to accomplish great feats of peace-making. (As an INTP, Carl Jung also had feeling as his inferior function, but for him it was extraverted feeling.)

Sensing as the Fourth Function

When sensing is one's inferior function, one must first practice the necessary self-discipline of the other three functions and make space in one's busy life for leisure, rest, and even play, if one wishes to activate one's inferior sensing function. Then one discovers the amazing sensation of being aware of new, living symbols that enable us to have direct experiences of God and spiritual, numinous reality while still on earth. Most probably the greatest mystics and contemplatives were persons with an inferior sensing function.

The special vocation of persons who have sensing as their inferior function, especially if they are the celebrant, or homilist, or music leader at a liturgy, is to activate this sensing function during liturgical and sacramental celebrations. If they are successful, not only will the liturgical symbols become alive and meaningful to them, but they will also set the stage for the symbols to become alive for the rest of the congregation who will experience a grace-filled liturgy. Actually, it behooves all of us to find the secret of activating the transcendent dimension of our sensing function, especially when we participate in any liturgical or sacramental celebration. To the extent we succeed in doing this, to that extent will we succeed in enlivening a liturgical celebration and making it the means for ourselves and others to have a deep spiritual experience of God's presence, grace, power, and love.

Intuition as the Fourth Function

Because intuition allows us to be able to see the inner substance of an event or happening, it enables one to see the potential more than the actual. Usually, at first, people who have intuition as their inferior function disregard the sudden, uninvited hunches and insights that occur to them. These are discounted as foolish, crazy, impractical ideas; for when the sensing function is one's dominant function, one takes great pride in being a very practical, down-to earth, sensible person. Each time their inferior intuitive function is activated, it is seen as a threat to the practical operation of their sensible life.

Only in the second half of life after the activation of one's tertiary function of thinking or feeling, does one have the courage to consider the inner world of ideas and the inspirations that the inferior intuitive function will suggest. After a careful valuing of these ideas for their merit by the wisdom of one's maturity, a person with an inferior intuitive function may become a prophet for their time. Once those who have intuition as their inferior function have attained the maturity that allows them to crystallize their intuitive function, they will be able to read the signs of the times and discern the direction that God wills for us to go on our journey of faith into the unknown future.

The Conversion of the Fourth Function

To the extent that we have succeeded in activating the transcendent dimension of each of the four functions, we will be able to use each function to accomplish great good in the world. During the second half of life, the inferior or fourth function can become a powerful, influential, and durable function if one has succeeded in learning the secret of how to activate it. This is revealed only to the extent that we have succeeded in actualizing or activating the inner Self. This inner center of our being, rather than our conscious will, has control over our inferior function. However, once the inferior function is activated, one's conscious will decides how to use the tremendous powers of the activated inferior function for good or for evil. Depending on what choice is made, an activated inferior function can do great good or great harm.

Most people tend to neglect the development of their fourth function because it is so difficult to control and use. Because functioning in its particular mode demands more psychic energy, one is apt to become tired, bored, or just lazy, and slip back into more familiar patterns, shying away from the less controllable fourth. Usually, we need to be well-rested, relaxed, calm, peaceful, and free of pressure and anxiety for the fourth function to operate well and usefully. Very often we learn to perform well in the fourth function when we are at some simple, childlike play or mild physical exercise such as gardening or taking a walk. A person who has learned how to relax in leisure and in life will usually be able to unlock the tremendous resources that lie hidden in the inferior function.

Centering prayer, contemplative prayer, and prayer of quiet are other ways that open the doors of the inferior function. Each person is different, so one needs to experiment by trying different ways until one finds the particular key to using one's inferior function. Even then, years of trial and error are usually required before we learn to use it well. We often feel that we are wasting a lot of valuable time just waiting until we can grasp the secret of the powerful inferior function. If we are patient and keep ourselves relaxed, well-rested, and at peace, the inferior function will suddenly surprise us with its valuable insights. We need to respect its moods and arrange our life to fit its schedule. If so, we will become more open to the inspirations of God's grace and thus allow the Holy Spirit to guide our life more completely.

Activating the Third and Fourth Functions in Prayer

Prayer is everything that helps our different relationships with God. Since God is a Spirit, the only way to have a direct encounter with God is by means of the spiritual dimension of our human nature. Whenever we touch spiritual values such as love, truth, goodness, beauty, unity, justice, etc., we have had a valid encounter with the reality of God. People speak of such encounters as numinous, or transcendent, experiences. Our ability to have such experiences is the meaning of the Biblical expression that we have been made in the image and likeness of God (Genesis 1:26).

The four normal paths by which we encounter God upon earth are the four cognitive functions of Sensing, Intuition, Thinking and Feeling. Every time the transcendent dimension of any of these functions is activated, we have had a valid experience of prayer, since we have come face-to-face with God through a new insight or a new image of the wonders of God.

Therefore, any time that we have a direct encounter with truth, justice, love, beauty, goodness, or unity, we are actually experiencing a certain union with God. Thus, even those people who claim to be atheists and non-believers have encounters with God without realizing or naming them. God is still God regardless of the name we choose to give these spiritual, transcendental phenomena during our life on earth. The highest of all these experiences of God upon earth is the understanding of love. As St. John states it: "God is love and anyone who abides in love, abides in God and God in them" (I John 4: 16).

There are many ways to activate the transcendent dimension of each of the four functions. Sometimes meditating or just considering one of the transcendental values mentioned above will activate the transcendent dimension of one or more of the four functions and bring us to an experience of encounter of God. Or, a successful experience of psychotherapy may activate the spiritual dimension of one or more of the psychological functions and lead us to a valid experience of God and prayer. The traditional ways of prayer are not the only successful ways of getting in touch with the spiritual and with God. In the past we made a distinction between nature and grace; actually, all of nature is filled with grace.

CHAPTER NINE

PRAYER SUGGESTIONS
FOR THE SIXTEEN
MBTI INDIVIDUAL TYPES

For some, taking the MBTI is easy and swift: they have complete certainty as to their preferences and thus no squabble with the final outcome. For others, it can be more difficult for a variety of reasons such as how they *wish* they were versus their true self; because of cultural, educational, or social pressure or conformity; or hesitancy, for whatever reason, to consider the possible traits attributed to a particular Type.

A person's score can also be ambiguous, falling in the middle with not a clear preference. In this country our social, educational, industrial, military, and governmental way of life is somewhat biased to the left side of the scale, i.e., Extravert, Sensing, Thinking, Judging Types. Therefore, if on the MBTI you score in the middle or if you had difficulty in deciding as to where you fit after reading descriptions of the attributes,[1] the likelihood is that your innate choice or preference is on the right side of the scale. After many years of research and consideration, Isabel Briggs Myers arrived at this conclusion. Her rationale was that those on the right side of the scale are forced to swim against the current of public approbation or acceptance, and so if one finds oneself caught in the middle, then the likelihood is that by nature we are inclined to the right side. In our experience, this conclusion has proved to be accurate in most situations where a person has difficulty deciding which side of a pair of preferences to choose.

We suggest reading through several, if not all, of the prayer suggestions to see what resonates with you and so that you may be equipped to assist others in their journey.

~ The Prayer of the ESTP ~

Basic Temperament – SP
Dominant – Sensation
Auxiliary – Thinking
Inferior – Intuition
Tertiary – Feeling

ESTPs are people of action, unpredictable, yet resourceful promoters, pragmatists. They, in truth, can say that their work is their prayer provided it is done for the glory of God and the welfare of their neighbor.

Keep in mind that for that work to be put in the right perspective, ESTPs must have a sincere and moral commitment to truth, to justice, to charity, and to the recognition of the personal value of others. Frequently it is difficult for this type to make a deep commitment, so this is the area in which they need to concentrate. Otherwise, they will make a god out of their own desires and ambitions for power. ESTPs often find it difficult to live under tension and so try to avoid stress at all costs, even by flight to some other place or concern. To overcome this temptation, they need a practical regime of regular self-discipline and self-sacrifice.

Besides praying while working, driving, etc., the ESTP needs at least a half hour of formal prayer and meditation each day. The *Lectio Divina* of St. Benedict is one recommended form for such daily prayer. This means spending a few minutes reading a passage of Sacred Scripture until a verse or short passage is found that speak to one's needs. Then perhaps 10 or 15 minutes should be spent in reflection on this passage in order to make application to oneself and to discover what God is trying to reveal. "What message is the Lord sending me?" "What is the Lord asking me to do?" "What change in my life is the Lord asking of me?" "What response should I make to the Word of the Lord?" The reflection should be the heart of the prayer period and should be followed by prayers of humility, contrition, gratitude, generosity, petition, praise, resolution, etc., as called for by the situation. Finally, at the end one should spend a few minutes to glorify and thank God for revealing His Word; then just be quiet and rest for a while in God's presence.

Centering prayer is a wonderful aid to the prayer-life of the ESTP. However, over the long haul, Franciscan types of prayer are apt to be the "bread and butter" prayers for most ESTPs. Spontaneous prayers and songs of praise and gratitude should be liberally sprinkled throughout the ESTP's day in order to help maintain a close union with God even in the midst of a busy work-day. When alone, prayers and songs may be recited or sung aloud.

Good experiences of community are essential to the spiritual growth of the ESTP and are normally found at weekly church services. However, if this is lacking, this time could be supplemented in a prayer group. ESTPs desire and need to share their faith journey with others and have others share their faith journey with them. The Cursillo is one example of where an ESTP can experience Christian community in its initial weekend retreat as well as the ongoing meetings. ESTPs usually enjoy singing and giving praise to God. It is important to practice this in a good Christian community setting.

Spiritual experiences of the ESTPs are usually concerned with the details of their own life, such as dramatic answers to personal prayers. They are frequently able to experience the presence of God, the love of God, and the protection of God. Some ESTPs also experience extra sensory perception (ESP) and deep, intuitive knowledge of persons and events even at a distance.

The books of the Bible that are attractive to the ESTP are the Canticles of Praise in the Old Testament (e.g., Daniel 3:26-90), Psalms of Praise, the Gospel of John, and the Gospel of Mark with its action oriented description of the life of Jesus.

Developing and Recognizing the Potential of the ESTP Shadow

Become familiar with the basic attributes of the INFJ personality, which is your opposite in type. Consider how you do not use your Inferior Function of Intuition and Tertiary Function of Feeling to the fullest. When reading the portrait of the INFJ type, what specifically struck you as so different from your customary way of acting and doing? During your period of prayer think about how these new attributes and ways of relating could be manifested in your daily living. Meditate prayerfully on each one of the qualities of the INFJ that you wish to acquire by using perhaps the Thomistic method of prayerful consideration, asking yourself the questions: what, why, how, when, where, who, with what helps?

The shadow qualities that the ESTP should consider at prayer, ponder upon, and act upon are reflected in some or all of the following suggestions.

- Practice more depth of concentration when considering each situation in life.
- Become aware of your own feelings; express them through warmth, understanding, compassion, sympathy.
- Be sensitive to the needs and feelings of others; try to overcome selfish tendencies and be considerate of the needs of others.
- Show as much warmth as possible in relationships with others.
- Learn to base decisions on personal value as well as on logic.
- Look beyond the facts at hand and consider possibilities and future potential
- Learn to live with tension and anxiety by deepening your trust in God and God's loving care.
- Plan, organize, and carry through to completion a major project.
- Be careful to complete a project that you have begun by personally taking care of the follow-up details and not by leaving them to someone else.
- Be faithful to commitments and relationships.
- Be a good listener, and do not pretend to know all that needs to be known.
- Learn to enjoy being alone at times.

~ The Prayer of the ISTP ~

Basic Temperament – SP
Dominant – Thinking
Auxiliary – Sensation
Inferior – Feeling
Tertiary – Intuition

ISTPs are very practical, precise, efficient, quiet, reserved, objective, factual. They are the artisans and craftsmen. They are good at exploration and usually possess tireless energy in pursuing the object of their search.

ISTPs prefer action over prayer and so will need to find ways of prayer that can be used while working. The Prayer of the Practice of the Presence of God (remembering that God is with us always) and the Jesus Prayer would be appropriate for this type. We recommend Brother Lawrence's *Practice of the Presence of God*[2] as a good book for study. It will help one to experience God in all the ordinary events of daily life.

Since they thrive on deep thinking and concentration, ISTPs need to spend at least 30 minutes daily in the practice of formal prayer. This may consist simply of just being silent and being with the Lord. They need orderly structure as well as self-discipline in order to profit most from both public and private prayer.

They must remember that spiritual experiences will also be found in the presence of a spirit-filled community such as a Cursillo or some other group with which the ISTP feels comfortable and completely at home. ISTPs also need appreciation and understanding from others and, therefore, need at least a trustworthy spiritual friend and companion, if not a larger group of like-minded friends, with whom they can share. ISTPs will benefit from belonging to a prayer group only if it is well conducted, orderly, and has good spiritual sharing.

The *Lectio Divina* of St. Benedict, Franciscan prayer, and the Spiritual Exercises of St. Ignatius are appropriate prayer forms for use during the formal prayer periods. ISTPs might use their sensible imagination to place themselves in the scenes of the Gospel, as St. Ignatius recommends, but at the end they always should try to draw some practical fruit from their meditation.

If the *Lectio Divina* is used, half of the prayer period should be spent in meditating on the meaning of the Scripture passage or spiritual reading. Probably only about five minutes should be spent in the actual reading at the beginning of the period. One should read just long enough to get some worthwhile thought upon which one should then dwell for the next 15 minutes. This should be followed by prayers of petition, humility, contrition, gratitude, resolution, commitment. Finally, a few quiet minutes should be taken before concluding to allow the new thoughts to sink more deeply into one's consciousness.

The Franciscan type of prayer is especially appealing to ISTPs. A suggestion for prayer is to imagine Jesus walking with you as you are in the country, or in a park, or around a lake, or by the ocean. "What might I say to Jesus and what might Jesus say to me?" The exchange should be totally free and spontaneous; this sort of setting and dialogue is especially appealing to the ISTPs.

ISTPs should feel free to try new and different ways of prayer and not become stuck in one form or method. In order to activate their Inferior Function of Feeling and their Tertiary Function of Intuition, Augustinian and Thomistic prayer forms should be used at least once a week. The more difficult type of prayer will be the Augustinian. The simpler the structure of their prayer, the more the ISTPs will benefit from it. ISTPs must learn to trust God to take care of things.

Recognizing and Developing the Potential of the ISTP Shadow

Become familiar with the basic attributes of the ENFJ personality, which is your opposite in type. Consider how you do not use your Inferior Function of Feeling and your Tertiary Function of Intuition to the fullest. When reading the portrait of the ENFJ type, what specifically struck you as so different from your customary way of acting and doing? During your period of prayer think about how these new attributes and ways of relating could be manifested in your daily living. Meditate prayerfully on each one of the qualities of the ENFJ that you wish to acquire by using perhaps the Thomistic method of prayerful consideration, asking yourself the questions: what, why, how, when, where, who, with what helps?

The shadow qualities that the ISTP should consider at prayer, ponder upon, and act upon are reflected in some or all of the following suggestions.

- Show warmth and sympathy for others; be friendly, tactful; develop the feeling side of your personality and learn to express feelings openly before others.
- Develop some close friendships and spend prime time each week with them.
- Feel responsible for others.
- Be faithful to promises and commitments.
- Be cooperative even though you do not feel like it or see no value to it.

- Try to see the value of the opinion of the other with whom you disagree; in a discussion mention points of agreement before plunging into points of disagreement.
- Be tolerant of those with whom you disagree.
- Be open to hunches, inspirations, insights, possibilities. Follow and explore some of them. Look for the potential good behind obvious facts.
- Be willing to follow the rules and regulations at work or elsewhere, even though they seem unnecessary but are what others desire.
- Work to create harmony at home, in the work-place, community.
- Volunteer to be a leader of some committee or group.
- Take time to prepare for some event, action, project; and then follow it through to the end.
- Make a schedule for next week and stick to it.
- Resume some routines that have been neglected.

~ The Prayer of the ESTJ ~

Basic Temperament – SJ
Dominant – Thinking
Auxiliary – Sensation
Inferior – Feeling
Tertiary – Intuition

ESTJs are responsible, orderly, realistic, matter-of-fact, conservative, consistent. The ESTJs like standard operating procedures and seek to preserve the established order. In their prayer life, they may prefer traditional prayers such as the Divine Office. However, they may find the Rosary difficult since they are unable to do two things at once: meditate on the Mystery and say the prayers. They may also become easily distracted with the monotonous repetition. Therefore, they should attempt to be more spontaneous and conversational during the time of private prayer.

For liturgy, ESTJ s prefer one that does not constantly change whether small weekly changes or large overhauls such as what occurred in the Catholic Church following Vatican II. Basically practical, law-and-order people, they will nevertheless follow the rules of the Church and be loyal to authority, even when interiorly they do not agree. ESTJs desire above all else to preserve the established order and keep the establishment healthy and balanced. They will resist any abrupt changes especially when they do not come from the properly constituted authority.

The ESTJ needs to spend a minimum of 30 minutes each day praying alone. During this period, they should try spontaneous prayer from the heart in addition to using words composed by someone else. The Spiritual Exercises of St. Ignatius could be of great help to the growth of their spiritual life. ESTJs should train themselves to use their sensible imagination to project themselves back into the Gospel scenes and imagine what Jesus might say to them and what they in turn might say to Jesus. As St. Ignatius recommends, they should strive to draw from these contemplations of the events in the life of Jesus some fruit to use in their own life.

The Thomistic method of logical consideration and meditation on virtues and faults may also be a useful form of prayer for the ESTJ. With its orderly progression from spiritual reading to meditation, prayer, and contemplation, the Benedictine *Lectio Divina* will appeal to the ESTJ.

ESTJs may find belonging to a prayer group helpful because of the sharing and support given and received. As extraverts they need the support of others to maintain a good prayer life and continual growth on their spiritual journey. Similarly, they need good experiences of community and congregational participation at Sunday liturgy for the Eucharist to be truly meaningful. Therefore, they should make it a priority to participate in a retreat such as Cursillo, and become part of a planning team. Such community spiritual experiences of prayer will be a rich source of spiritual growth for the ESTJ.

If ESTJs will take the time to pray each day, they may expect deep comfort, support, help, and a sense of resting in the loving care of God, which will result in an inner peace and a feeling of closeness to God. Such experiences may happen very suddenly but rarely in the course of life; but the comfort and strength received from these moments of grace will enable the ESTJ to persevere along the path to holiness and salvation. ESTJs should strive to keep themselves open to the presence of the Holy Spirit and be ever willing to change the direction of their life in order to bring it more into conformity with the will of God.

Augustinian prayer will probably be the most difficult for the ESTJ since it requires the use of their Inferior and Tertiary Functions, but it is highly recommended that they use this type of prayer at least once a week. Franciscan prayer forms may not seem real prayers to them, but if used they too will prove of great spiritual benefit.

Recognizing and Developing the Potential of the ESTJ Shadow

Become familiar with the basic attributes of the INFP personality, which is your opposite in type. Consider how you do not use your Inferior Function of Feeling and your Tertiary Function of Intuition to the fullest. When reading the portrait of the INFP type, what specifically struck you as so different from your customary way of acting and doing? During your period of prayer think about how these new attributes and ways of relating could be manifested in your daily living. Meditate prayerfully on each one of the qualities of the INFP that you wish to acquire by using perhaps the Thomistic method of prayerful consideration, asking yourself the questions: what, why, how, when, where, who, with what helps?

The shadow qualities that the ESTJ should consider at prayer, ponder upon, and act upon are reflected in some or all of the following suggestions.

- Follow feelings, impulses, hunches rather than logic and reasoning.
- Find joy in pleasing others; be sensitive to the feelings of others.
- Show appreciation for other's merits; praise, compliment, affirm others; refer more often to what is well done than to what needs correction.
- Develop and express your feelings to others, especially to your family, spouse, and children.
- Show enthusiasm, warmth, sympathy for others.
- Do not jump to conclusions about others.
- Reserve judgment and avoid hasty judgments.
- Listen to other people's point of view, especially of those who ordinarily are not in a position to talk back.

- Show patience with those who do not carry out all details of a project.
- Study some topic for which you see no practical use but which you undertake just for the sake of learning.
- Look for possibilities and undeveloped potential for good.
- Keep one day a week unstructured, unplanned, open-ended. Go for a trip, or take off a day or afternoon, without having any previously made plans for its organization.
- Be open to ways and points of view other than your own.
- Be willing to deviate from your usual "standard operating procedures."
- Be a follower sometimes and do what others want rather than what you want.

~ The Prayer of the ISTJ ~

Basic Temperament – SJ
Dominant – Sensation
Auxiliary – Thinking
Inferior – Intuition
Tertiary – Feeling

ISTJs are serious, quiet, thorough, orderly, logical, matter-of-fact. They are duty-oriented and no-nonsense persons who like everything organized, proper, straight-forward. They are the guardians of time-honored institutions, resistant to change, and conservative by nature. They find it difficult to handle strong feelings and emotions and so may give the impression of having ice in their veins when a decision has to be made. They can be pillars of strength for any institution and, with their strong convictions, can be charismatic leaders. Saint John Paul II was most likely an ISTJ-type.

Being introverted, the ISTJ needs to spend substantial time alone with God each day. Since St. Ignatius was also likely an ISTJ, it would seem the Spiritual Exercises would be appropriate and appealing to the ISTJ temperament. The ISTJ should aim to develop the sensible imagination in order to project oneself back into the scenes of the Scripture as participant. For, example, St. Ignatius suggests that one should imagine oneself to be as servant, present in the stable at the birth of Jesus, allowed to hold the Baby Jesus and listen to the conversation between Mary and Joseph and the shepherds. Ignatius always ends each of his meditations with the advice: "And draw some practical fruit from the contemplation."

The *Lectio Divina* of St. Benedict, with its progression from spiritual reading, to meditation, oration, and finally contemplation, will also provide an orderly format for the prayer of the ISTJ. The books of the Bible especially useful to the ISTJ would be the Gospel of St. Matthew, Isaiah, Acts, Psalms, Exodus, Numbers, and Deuteronomy. There is a great need for the ISTJ to learn the technique and develop the "art of listening" to God through the Scriptures or otherwise. Therefore, a directed retreat using the Spiritual Exercises might be very helpful as a means to learn and develop this practice of listening to God.

In order to activate the transcendent dimension of their Inferior and Tertiary Functions, the ISTJs should try to use Augustinian prayer at least once a week. This will help to develop their Feeling and Intuition Functions which otherwise will remain repressed and undifferentiated. Thomistic and Franciscan prayer forms should come somewhat easier to them and should also be used at least once weekly.

Because of their structure, both the Divine Office and the Rosary may be found helpful. The ISTJ may like set formulae of prayer but may feel the need to change them every few months or oftener in order to prevent routine from destroying their union with God.

The ISTJs find great fulfillment in praying alone, but their highlighted prayer experiences will usually come through community or congregational experiences. Therefore, we recommend participating in community-focused retreats and finding a small group of like-minded friends with whom to meet, pray and reflect on a weekly basis. The ISTJ needs the support of a vibrant and faith-filled community.

Since they usually find it difficult to express their feelings and to grasp or describe any deep spiritual experiences, it may be well for ISTJs to try keeping a spiritual journal. Writing in a journal would further the development of two faculties: their basic orderliness and their need for recall of their progression in the spiritual life.

The ISTJ can expect a sense of satisfaction that comes from conscientiously doing the will of God as revealed through their conscience. Among the faith experiences that may come to the ISTJ will be experiences of God 's loving care and support as a clear answer to prayer, experiences of contrition for past sins and God's loving forgiveness, and experiences of conversion and change in one's spiritual life.

Recognizing and Developing the Potential of the ISTJ Shadow

Become familiar with the basic attributes of the ENFP personality, which is your opposite in type. Consider how you do not use your Inferior Function of Intuition and Tertiary Function of Feeling to the fullest. When reading the portrait of the ENFP type, what specifically struck you as so different from your customary way of acting and doing? During your period of prayer think about how these new attributes and ways of relating could be manifested in your daily living. Meditate prayerfully on each one of the qualities of the ENFP that you wish to acquire by using perhaps the Thomistic method of prayerful consideration, asking yourself the questions: what, why, how, when, where, who, with what helps?

The shadow qualities that the ISTJ should consider at prayer, ponder upon, and act upon are reflected in some or all of the following suggestions.

- Act occasionally on impulse.
- Look for new ways of doing things rather than the old, accustomed ways.
- Be open to future potential and possibilities.
- Try to develop a greater breadth of interest.
- Take extra pains to understand others and appreciate them.
- Make a special effort to relate to others.
- Be generous in giving thanks, praise, compliments, appreciation, affirmation to other people.
- Practice patience with others who do not see things as you do or who are not dependable.
- Show more warmth, feeling, understanding, consideration for the feelings of others.
- Make a deliberate attempt to be talkative (without the help of alcohol) when at some gathering of people.

- Be warmly enthusiastic about something.
- Take a day or afternoon off without planning anything ahead of time.

~ The Prayer of the ESFP ~

Basic Temperament – SP
Dominant – Sensation
Auxiliary – Feeling
Inferior – Intuition
Tertiary – Thinking

ESFPs are born leaders, good entertainers, very attractive personalities, and easily attract a large following. People enjoy having them around. Wherever they go, they bring warmth, enthusiasm, optimism. ESFPs are the life of the party and love excitement. They are impulsive, frequently putting their foot in the wrong place.

The important thing for this temperament is to be with people and to be a part of the action. ESFPs will find a prayer group enjoyable because of the companionship and encouragement of the group. ESFPs will enjoy any type of community retreat and add much to its success. They are generous and willing to accept people and things as they are and make the best of them. They love to be of service to others and are capable of the grand gesture of generosity, be it for God or for their fellow human beings.

ESFPs will probably find the externals of religion a help to their spiritual growth: lighted candles, crucifixes, sacred pictures, statues, incense, etc. They may be rather impulsive in their spiritual life, doing things and making gestures like long fasts and all-night vigils. Dramatic Franciscan type of prayers will usually be their preferred form of prayer along with spontaneous prayers of praise and gratitude.

It is important, however, that ESFPs should also find time each day to pray alone and connect with God. Thirty minutes every day should be spent speaking and listening to God such as in the *Lectio Divina* of St. Benedict. Begin with spiritual reading of the Bible or some other book on matters religious, then meditate and reflect on its meaning, search for an application to oneself of what has been read. Finally, close with thanksgiving for the insights received, resolution of amendment, and some quiet time to bask in the goodness, love, glory, and beauty of God.

ESFPs are able to identify with the Passion of Christ quite well and therefore may find the Sorrowful Mysteries of the Rosary helpful. They are extremely generous in their willingness to sacrifice themselves for others. The Canticles of Praise scattered throughout the Old Testament, especially the Canticle of the Three Hebrew Youths in the fiery furnace (Daniel 3:26-90), will probably strike a responsive chord in their hearts. St. Francis' Canticle of the Sun and other similar prayers of praise of God's creation are most rewarding prayers for the ESFP temperament. The temperament of St. Francis of Assisi was most likely ESFP.

ESFPs often experience God through direct, dramatic answers to their prayers of intercession. They also, like St. Francis, feel and experience God in nature, especially the animate nature of plants and animals. It is very much to their advantage to practice the needed discipline of exposing themselves to all the other types of prayer: Thomistic, Augustinian, and Ignatian.

Recognizing and Developing the Potential of the ESFP Shadow

Become familiar with the basic attributes of the INTJ personality, which is your opposite in type. Consider how you do not use your Inferior Function of Intuition and your Tertiary Function of Thinking to the fullest. When reading the portrait of the INTJ, what specifically struck you as so different from your customary way of acting and doing? During your period of prayer, think about how these new attributes and ways of relating could be manifested in your daily living. Meditate prayerfully on each of the qualities of the INTJ that you wish to acquire by using perhaps the Thomistic method of prayerful consideration, asking yourself the questions: what, why, how, when, where, who, with what helps?

The shadow qualities that the ESFP should consider at prayer, ponder upon, and act upon are reflected in some or all of the following suggestions.

- Learn to trust intuitions, hunches, flashes of thoughts.
- Learn to trust new ideas, and be willing to take the risk of introducing them.
- Develop a single-mindedness in pursuit of some goal or objective.
- Try to establish a balanced view that considers both negative and positive, dark and bright sides, of a situation, problem, or decision.
- Develop the willingness to act alone and be alone for some worthwhile project.
- Develop the psychic strength to tackle something that looks seemingly impossible.

- Show a decisiveness and single-mindedness about some important topic and even about the direction of one's own life.
- Work on developing a logical approach that analyzes a situation before deciding.
- Take the responsibility for organizing and seeing to completion some project.
- Consider the long-term consequences of your actions and decisions.

~ The Prayer of the ISFP ~

Basic Temperament – SP
Dominant – Feeling
Auxiliary – Sensation
Inferior – Thinking
Tertiary – Intuition

ISFPs are free spirits, who desire to follow the guidance of the Holy Spirit and impulse of the moment. They are capable of a great intensity of feeling and have an eye for detail. Endowed with artistic ability, they are lovers of nature. The beauties of nature speak to them of God, God's power, God's presence, God's beauty, God's goodness, and God's loving care.

At Eucharist ISFPs enjoy joyful congregational singing; good experiences of community and a prayerful, enthusiastic, spirit-filled celebrant make their Sunday Mass most profitable and enjoyable. Similarly, an intensive weekend retreat such as a Cursillo, is recommended. ISFPs will enjoy sharing the fellowship, singing and praising of God, in a prayer group.

Prayer forms for this type need to be flexible to allow the ISFP to go in whatever direction the Spirit leads. However, they must not allow this to prevent them from spending at least 30 minutes each day in prayerful reflection to allow a real contact with the Holy Spirit and to put their life in a balanced order. For this to happen, they must maintain discipline in their life especially in giving prime time each day to listening to God in prayerful reflection. The Benedictine *Lectio Divina* of spiritual reading, reflection, prayer, and contemplation will be very helpful in this regard.

ISFPs need to speak to God from the heart regarding whatever they happen to be thinking about or trying to decide. ISFPs must keep their mind and heart open to any new inspirations of the Holy Spirit. Using a daily spiritual journal to communicate with God is an excellent method to maintain this intimate contact with God, the Holy Spirit, and Jesus.

ISFPs can expect experiences of God's presence that are real and deep and sometimes quite awesome. They need assurances of God's personal love for them, and normally God is not reluctant to give them a sensible experience of His presence and loving care. God seems to favor them especially with answers to prayers for both inner and bodily healings of self and others. The Baptism of the Holy Spirit, through the laying on of hands by a prayer group, is often a very real and vivid experience for ISFPs.

An appropriate Scripture passage for ISFPs would be: "Rejoice in the Lord always! Again, I say, rejoice! Let everyone see how unselfish you are. The Lord is near. Dismiss all anxiety from your minds. Present your needs to God in every form of prayer and petitions full of gratitude. Then God's own peace, which is beyond all understanding, will stand guard over your hearts and minds, in Christ Jesus" (Philippians 4:4-7).

ISFPs will find most appealing the Franciscan type of prayer of spontaneous praise and gratitude. However, Ignatian and

Augustinian prayer forms, as well as *Lectio Divina*, will also be valuable and useful for them. Only the Thomistic type of prayer will be found difficult; but effort should be made to use this form of prayer when well-rested and lots of leisure time is available. If so used, the transcendent dimension of their Inferior Function will suddenly reveal to them beautiful new insights into divine truth. Thus, they are able to simplify what previously had seemed quite confused and complex. Once successfully experienced. Thomistic prayer will also become attractive to them. Their spirituality, because of their artistic and free spirit, may be expressed in some external form of sensible art: music, painting, dance, flower arranging, sculpture.

Recognizing and Developing the Potential of The ISFP Shadow

Become familiar with the basic attributes of the ENTJ personality, which is your opposite in type. Consider how you do not use your Inferior Function of Thinking and Tertiary Function of Intuition to the fullest. When reading the portrait of the ENTJ type, what specifically struck you as so different from your customary way of acting and doing? During your period of prayer think about how these new attributes and ways of relating could be manifested in your daily living. Meditate prayerfully on each one of the qualities of the ENTJ that you wish to acquire by using perhaps the Thomistic method of prayerful consideration, asking yourself the questions: what, why, how, when, where, who, with what helps?

The shadow qualities that the ISFP should consider at prayer, ponder upon, and act upon are reflected in some or all of the following suggestions.

- Organize and carry through some project – Set goals and objectives ahead of time; prepare a schedule; develop a timeframe; and then try to stick to the schedule.
- Be persevering and stubborn in following through some project or idea.
- Take some task that requires you to work under pressure to meet a deadline.
- Endeavor to be logical in analyzing and reasoning.
- Try to convince someone who does not agree with you; be willing to disagree; yet stick to your convictions openly as well as silently.
- Select a subject for study and persevere until a good grasp of it has been attained.
- Start a savings account at the bank.
- Seek an opportunity to do public speaking.
- Talk about your accomplishments in public as well as in private.
- Be willing to be in the limelight or center of attention even if for only a brief amount of time.

~ The Prayer of the ESFJ ~

Basic Temperament – SJ
Dominant – Feeling
Auxiliary – Sensation
Inferior – Thinking
Tertiary – Intuition

The ESFJ person is the most sociable of all the types. They find it easy to make friends with even total strangers. Sympathetic, their emotions are very close to the surface at all times. Out-going, soft-hearted, sentimental, they need to be loved and noticed and appreciated. They are very giving, caring, comforting. They need and seek harmony and are strongly affected by the opinion of others.

ESFJs love to pray in groups and find prayer groups quite helpful to spiritual growth. Since they love to pray and sing in groups, they usually enjoy charismatic prayer groups with praising, singing, and uninhibited expression of emotions. They do not mind long prayers.

The ESFJ needs to learn to talk to God as if He were a friend. Intercessory prayers[3] for others should form a substantial part of their prayer life. Their needs, problems, their friends, and others in need should be the subject of their conversations with God. Praise, gratitude, humility, and petitions should be present in a proper balance. Using a spiritual journal to write a letter to Jesus each day would be another way for the ESFJ to talk to God.

Since ESFJs tend to do all the talking when in prayer, special effort to learn and practice the skill of "listening" to God should be made. The four parts of *Lectio Divina* would be most helpful in this regard. After some reading of the Scriptures or other religious writings, ESFJs should meditate and reflect upon the lessons therein, seeking to discern God's will for them in the reading; then gratitude, praise, and petition, or resolution and commitment may follow with some quiet time to contemplate and enjoy the goodness of God.

The Scriptures most useful to the ESFJ will be the Psalms, the historical books of the Old Testament, the four Gospels, Acts, Epistle of James, First Epistle of John. ESFJs should be able to put to good use all forms of prayer: Ignatian, Franciscan, Augustinian. Ignatian and Franciscan should be the two favorite forms of prayer for the ESFJ, although some ESFJs have difficulty with the structuring and discipline required for the Ignatian type. The

Thomistic-type of prayer will require the most effort but can also be very rewarding when one is well-rested and will give it the needed time.

The Jesus Prayer, "Lord Jesus Christ, have mercy on me," may well become a favorite that can be repeated many times during the day. The Rosary can also be used profitably by this type. As far as possible the ESFJ should strive to live consciously in God's presence and use spontaneous prayer to evoke this continual presence of a loving God. ESFJs can rather easily center their heart on God and thus remain in the presence of God and prayer all day long.

ESFJs can expect many feelings of joy, peace, happiness while praying and should see these as authentic spiritual experiences of the presence of God in their lives. Apt to experience God through frequent answers to their prayers of intercession, they may also experience an emptiness which alternates with a feeling of closeness to God. Both are true spiritual experiences to remind them of the need of God and their total dependence upon Him. ESFJs should be grateful for every experience of God's presence, support, love, and help.

Recognizing and Developing the Potential of the ESFJ Shadow

Become familiar with the basic attributes of the INTP personality, which is your opposite in type. Consider how you do not use your Inferior Function of Thinking and Tertiary Function of Intuition to the fullest. When reading the portrait of the INTP type, what specifically struck you as so different from your customary way of acting and doing? During your period of prayer think about how these new attributes and ways of relating could be manifested in your daily living. Meditate prayerfully on each one of the qualities of the INTP that you wish to acquire by using perhaps the Thomistic method of prayerful consideration, asking yourself the questions: what, why, how, when, where, who, with what helps?

The shadow qualities that the ESFJ should consider at prayer, ponder upon, and act upon are reflected in some or all of the following suggestions.

- Look on the bright, optimistic side of things rather than only the dark and worst possibilities.
- Spend some time alone every day; perhaps make a silent, directed retreat.
- Spend some time thinking about your own worth as a person and individual.
- Face up to some disagreeable facts about yourself, your family, the community, and the world.
- Do some abstract, logical, objective thinking on some subject.
- Be willing to disagree openly with someone and even argue over it.
- Pursue study of some religious topic until you have full grasp of it.
- Try to practice flexibility and open-mindedness.
- Deviate from your regular routine at home for a full week, or even a month.
- Be generous – give to the poor until it hurts.

~ The Prayer of the ISFJ ~

Basic Temperament – SJ
Dominant – Sensation
Auxiliary – Feeling
Inferior – Intuition
Tertiary – Thinking

ISFJs are super-dependable, have a strong sense of duty, and usually relate well to people. They have a good sense of history and continuity and therefore may be conservative by nature. They love to minister to the needs of others and so are often overworked, imposed upon, and taken for granted. Because of their introverted tendency to avoid the limelight, they are often undervalued. Therefore, they are frequently taken advantage of by selfish, unthinking people and not appreciated for what they do.

ISFJs show an intense seriousness of purpose and a great generosity in pursuing whatever goal or ideal they choose. Among those who responded to the Prayer Project, the ISFJs outnumbered any other type of personality. This indicates their desire to want to please God and find the best way of praying to God.

The ISFJ likes to pray alone (introvert) and enjoys silent prayer. For spiritual growth, the ISFJ will find it necessary to spend a minimum of 30 to 60 minutes each day in prayer. The technique of "listening" to God as He speaks in the depths of one's heart should be developed. Either the Ignatian method of active, sensible imagination as explained in the Spiritual Exercises of St. Ignatius or the Benedictine *Lectio Divina* are suitable methods of prayer for the ISFJ.

Many ISFJs are not attracted to the Rosary. They especially do not like the public, group recitation of the Rosary but may find value in it when they recite it privately. The Franciscan type of spontaneous praying from the heart throughout the day will feed their spiritual hunger for God; however, they must realize that it is not necessary to verbalize their prayers. "The Holy Spirit helps us in our weakness; for we do not know how to pray as we ought, but the Spirit himself makes intercession for us with groanings that cannot be expressed in speech. He who searches hearts knows what the Spirit means, for the Spirit intercedes for the saints as God himself wills" (Romans 8:26-27).

ISFJs may be attracted to traditional forms of prayer and use a prayer book or prayers composed by others. ISFJs also enjoy using prayers, or mantras, mumbled under their breath as they go about their daily duties. They enjoy prayers of praise, gratitude, and love. Their spiritual life and prayers may at times be sentimental, but quietly so, since ISFJs may be reluctant to display their emotions in public. This shyness may disappear when they are part of a large group like a charismatic prayer meeting.

It is recommended that ISFJs participate in a Cursillo weekend and serve on a Cursillo team. This would furnish them the opportunity to have good faith experiences and a good Christian community for sharing and fellowship. It would also break through the wall sometimes built up around their feelings.

Since they live their religious life primarily in the external world, they may not even be aware of any mystical experiences; but they do experience specific answers to their prayers and may at times have real and vivid experiences of the presence of God in their lives. Indeed, some of the ISFJs who participated in the Prayer Project reported how they felt very close to the Lord, were moved to tears by a song or a scene in nature, experience a real visible image of Jesus, and felt the fullness of the Holy Spirit.

The most difficult prayer for the ISFJ is Thomistic since it requires the use of their Inferior and Tertiary Functions. Some find Franciscan prayer not prayerful enough because of its lack of structure. Some also have difficulty activating their sensible imagination sufficiently to use the Ignatian Spiritual Exercises. However, the needed discipline should be exercised to develop a familiarity with all these types of prayer. If so done, ISFJs will find their spiritual life greatly enriched.

Recognizing and Developing the Potential of the ISFJ Shadow

Become familiar with the basic attributes of the ENTP personality, which is your opposite in type. Consider how you do not use your Inferior Function of Intuition and Tertiary Function of Thinking to the fullest. When reading the portrait of the ENTP type, what specifically struck you as so different from your customary way of acting and doing? During your period of prayer think about how these new attributes and ways of relating could be manifested in your daily living. Meditate prayerfully on each one of the qualities of the ENTP that you wish to acquire by using perhaps the Thomistic method of prayerful consideration, asking yourself the questions: what, why, how, when, where, who, with what helps?

The shadow qualities that the ISFJ should consider at prayer, ponder upon, and act upon are reflected in some or all of the following suggestions.

- Develop good judgment by logical analysis of each situation.
- Be open to change and show a willingness to experiment and try new things.

- Develop a new hobby, or start doing something that is completely different from your customary activities. For instance, take up tennis, jog, attend socials.
- Break away from some routines in your life for—push yourself as to how long but make it more than a day.
- Follow your impulses much more frequently as long as your common sense tells you that the impulse is not sinful or wrong.
- Be more outspoken with the other members of your family than you have been in the past.
- Show some ingenuity in the way you solve a problem and be willing to risk failure or embarrassment.
- Be innovative, adventuresome; take risks; try new things.

~ The Prayer of the ENFP ~

Basic Temperament – NF
Dominant – Intuition
Auxiliary – Feeling
Inferior – Sensation
Tertiary – Thinking

Usually optimistic, ENFPs are warmly enthusiastic, imaginative, non-conformist. Their intuitive powers are quite strong, and they frequently experience extrasensory perception (ESP). Warm and sympathetic, they are usually skilled in handling people. Their extraversion tends to be well-developed, as is their attraction to the novel and dramatic.

For ENFPs, prayer is a necessity for survival, and they should allocate an hour each day for it. This hour may be spent in any, or all, of the four aspects of *Lectio Divina* spiritual reading of Scripture or other religious books; meditation and reflection on what has been read; prayers of petition, praise, gratitude, or contrition; contemplation on the beauties of God. ENFPs may find it profitable to use the prayers of different biblical personalities, e.g., the Canticles of Moses, Daniel, Mary, Elizabeth, Paul, and Jesus. Isaiah, the Song of Songs, the Psalms, the Gospels (particularly Luke and John), and the Pauline Epistles will speak most to the ENFP in prayerful reflection. ENFPs need to pray alone; but, more than other temperaments, they need the help of a community or prayer companion in order to pray. Therefore, good community experiences in liturgy are essential if the Eucharist is to be profitable to ENFPs.

ENFPs usually dislike repetitive prayer and find it better to use spontaneous prayer rising from the heart. Being extraverted, there is a tendency for ENFPs to want to do most or all of the talking when at prayer. Therefore, it is important that the ENFP spends at least half of the time listening and trying to discern what God wishes to say to them. ENFPs quite often have deep spiritual experiences of the presence of God or other spiritual presences. Such mystical experiences may occur at the time of prayer, at liturgy, or other times. They may feel a presence which reaches out and touches them or is a partner with them in a celebration of joy and elation. ENFPs need to especially work at developing good skills for interpreting the insights that come to them in prayer or from the words of the Bible. "Be still and listen" should be their motto.

ENFPs may enjoy the Rosary if it is kept flexible to accommodate their different moods and thoughts. However, on the whole, ENFPs often find it difficult to make use of their sensible imagination in prayer. This will explain the problem they have in using the Ignatian Spiritual Exercises. Unless the director modifies them to meet the needs of the ENFP personality, the 30-Day Spiritual Exercises of St. Ignatius may be too much for them. The Augustinian-type of prayer is especially appropriate for the needs of the ENFP personality. ENFPs can take a Scripture Passage and apply it with facility to their own life or the living situation of people in today's world.

ENFPs need to put some structure into their prayer life which otherwise will break down or evaporate. They should set a timetable for completion of projects since they have a propensity for procrastination of anything that is difficult and requires prolonged effort. However, too much structure will inhibit their prayerful union with God, so a proper balance must be struck. ENFPs must take care not to get themselves overloaded with activities; for as a result, they may end up going in circles and accomplishing little or nothing.

Recognizing and Developing the Potential of the ENFP Shadow

Become familiar with the basic attributes of the ISTJ personality, which is your opposite in type. Consider how you do not use your Inferior Function of Sensing and Tertiary Function of Thinking to the fullest. When reading the portrait of the ISTJ type, what specifically struck you as so different from your customary way of acting and doing? During your period of prayer think about how these new attributes and ways of relating could be manifested in your daily living. Meditate prayerfully on each one of the qualities of the ISTJ that you wish to acquire by using perhaps the Thomistic method of prayerful consideration, asking yourself the questions: what, why, how, when, where, who, with what helps?

The shadow qualities that the ENFP should consider at prayer, ponder upon, and act upon are reflected in some or all of the following suggestions.

- Reflect and concentrate more on developing the inner life of the spirit.
- Practice self-discipline, self-denial, fasting in some way.
- Be realistic, practical, patient with painstaking details.
- Deliberately carry out some routine tasks that you hate to do each day.
- Be thoroughly systematic in all you do for the next month.
- Follow "standard operating procedures" in some are of your life.
- Plan and organize a project, set a schedule for completion and then follow it through to completion.
- Develop a better eye for detail and memory of facts.
- Make a deliberate attempt to use logical analysis in solving some problem.
- Be open to the ideas of others and willing to forego your own plans in order accomplish some project.
- Be patient with those who disagree with you.
- Be faithful to your word, promise, commitment; show reliability and stability.

~ The Prayer of the INFP ~

Basic Temperament – NF
Dominant – Feeling
Auxiliary – Intuition
Inferior – Thinking
Tertiary – Sensation

INFPs have a great desire to pray alone and silently. An hour of formal prayer each day, set aside exclusively for God, is a must for INFPs. All four aspects of *Lectio Divina* may be used profitably by the INFP: spiritual reading; reflection on the new insights discovered in this reading; spontaneous prayer of gratitude, humility, petition, etc.; contemplation on the beauties of God or just resting quietly in His presence.

Because of this need of prayer, INFPs are constantly searching for new and better ways of prayer; and most INFPs have been in a prayer group. However, because they are introverted intuitives, flexible and open to new ideas, most typical prayer groups do not fulfill their requirements for prayer; they find that more quiet time than provided by the normal group meeting is essential. Therefore, they usually abandon such groups and seek other more individualistic ways.

INFPs should read short, appropriate passages of the Bible, try to apply them to their situation, and then discern what the Lord is revealing to them in the passage. This is the Augustinian method of prayer. Long passages of Scripture should not be read during prayer. This is appropriate for a devout study of the Bible but not during prayer time. The favorite books of the Bible for the INFP temperament are: Second Isaiah, the Psalms, the Gospels, and the Pauline Epistles. Once the INFP discovers an appropriate Scripture passage, this may be used again and again during the daily prayer period. The INFP should never be in a hurry to go to the next verse or another Scripture passage but should linger prayerfully over each verse or phrase or word as long as possible.

INFPs usually dislike set forms of prayer and prefer a more personal, spontaneous response to God. INFPs like to look at prayer not as a formal duty but rather as a time of joyful communion with one's most beloved friend: Jesus, or God the Father, or the Holy Spirit. They need to take time just to sit and be still and wait for the Lord to make known His will to them. This will result in experiences of a deep union of love with God and with the whole world.

INFPs can expect to have many close encounters with God during prayer. These faith experiences often bring a warmth of the presence of God into their lives. An over-powering sense of God's loving care may come in times of deep anguish, fear, trouble. A feeling of being carried out of one's self into the arms of God is sometimes experienced by INFPs. Another spiritual experience of INFPs is a feeling of deep attraction to God and a sense of divine providence or the loving and constant care of a merciful God. This leads to a deep trust in God.

INFPs need to be open and receptive to whatever the Lord wants of them. A requisite for them is to take seriously any hunch, intuition, or inspiration that comes to them. These should be submitted to their common sense or to the judgment of a spiritual friend or advisor who is trustworthy. These inspirations will sometimes come by way of dreams. A journal recording their dreams and their spiritual and temporal progression will help the INFP if it is kept unstructured and seen as a way of conversing with God and keeping a record of the new ideas or insights that come while reading, or praying, or just thinking.

Since there is a real danger of the INFP becoming too introverted, or too self-centered, INFPs must make a special effort every day to forget themselves and reach out to others. The INFP must not wait until whole and healed before reaching out to heal and help others. The INFP should begin their day with: "What can I do today to make others happier and better for having met me?"

Recognizing and Developing the Potential of the INFP Shadow

Become familiar with the basic attributes of the ESTJ personality, which is your opposite in type. Consider how you do not use your Inferior Function of Thinking and Tertiary Function of Sensing to the fullest. When reading the portrait of the ESTJ type, what specifically struck you as so different from your customary way of acting and doing? During your period of prayer think about how these new attributes and ways of relating could be manifested in your daily living. Meditate prayerfully on each one of the qualities of the ESTJ that you wish to acquire by perhaps using the Thomistic method of prayerful consideration, asking yourself the questions: what, why, how, when, where, who, with what helps?

The shadow qualities that the INFP should consider at prayer, ponder upon, and act upon are reflected in some or all of the following suggestions.

- Practice logical thinking and rational analysis of a situation in order to discover the unifying symbol or point that is common to all. Do this when well rested and with plenty of leisure time to allow the Inferior Thinking Function to operate.
- Use "standard operating procedures" more often than you are accustomed to doing.
- Plan and organize some project and personally carry it through to completion.
- Be consistent and follow through on a project even when it is no longer interesting.

- Be practical, realistic, matter-of -fact, factually-minded, with an eye for detail. Try to remember individual facts and details. Keep in touch with external realities.

- Do a good job of some worthwhile task which is very low on the list of your personal priorities, perhaps foregoing something else in which you are more interested.

- Be willing to give up your own ideas for the good of others, or at least delay their execution until the time is more suitable and agreeable to others.

- Practice some routine details in living that would give pleasure to others.

- Be open to interruptions from others even when it seems unnecessary and unimportant.

- Be willing to express feelings and even deeply felt emotions.

- Be interested in the past as well as in future possibilities.

~ The Prayer of the ENFJ ~

Basic Temperament – NF
Dominant – Feeling
Auxiliary – Intuition
Inferior – Thinking
Tertiary – Sensation

The ENFJ needs to take time each day to pray alone; if at all possible, 60 minutes would be recommended. During this time, the ENFJ should develop the habit of spending half of the prayer-time listening to God and trying to discern God's will. All four steps of St. Benedict's *Lectio Divina* should be used: reading, meditation, prayer, contemplation. Once the "listening" has discerned the direction of God's will, spontaneous prayer, spoken from the heart in a conversational manner, should be an important part of the ENFJs response to God's word. This is the Oratio of *Lectio Divina*.

The ENFJ needs good experiences of community at Eucharist and other public liturgical services. This will be fostered by robust congregational singing and other elements of good liturgy. The ENFJ may benefit from participating in a community-focused retreat, even taking on a leadership role such as on a Cursillo team, and belonging to a prayer group which meets regularly. Whatever the size of the prayer group, more than likely the ENFJ will, again, assume much of the responsibility for its leadership, since the ENFJ is the most natural leader of all sixteen types of personality. Such leadership may be assumed subtly even when someone else is nominal head of the group, or when no one is actually named as head.

ENFJs do not find the Rosary a prayerful experience because of the monotonous repetition. However, some of them find the recitation of the Rosary, or a mantra or repetitive prayer, has a soothing and calming effect when they are agitated. ENFJs should use their personal freedom to experiment with different forms of prayer and different reading material until they find the form or material appropriate for the occasion. ENFJs usually have the ability to use many different types of prayer, and they should make good use of this facility. Usually the Augustinian-type of prayer will be preferred. However, with a little effort, the ENFJ is usually able to adopt all the other methods of prayer with much spiritual profit. Thomistic prayer will be the most difficult and require the most effort.

ENFJs can expect even dramatic answers to prayer if their prayer is intense. Many ENFJs find that they have been given the charismatic gift of healing of others through the laying-on of hands. ENFJs should be generous in their willingness to use whatever gifts God may have given them keeping in mind that "Nothing is impossible with God" (Luke1:37) and that "All things are possible to those who believe" (Mark 9:23).

ENFJs can trust their intuitions, hunches, and sudden ideas which will pop into their minds. They will usually be on target; however, they should be submitted to the judgment of their common sense. Because of the ENFJ's immense powers for either good or evil, it is imperative that the ENFJ be most unselfish in serving others. The constant pre-occupation of the ENFJ should be: "How can I do the most good for the most people?"

Recognizing and Developing the Potential of the ENFJ Shadow

Become familiar with the basic attributes of the ISTP personality, which is your opposite in type. Consider how you do not use your Inferior Function of Thinking and Tertiary Function of Sensing to the fullest. When reading the portrait of the ISTP type, what specifically struck you as so different from your customary way of acting and doing? During your period of prayer think about how these new attributes and ways of relating could be manifested in your daily living. Meditate prayerfully on each one of the qualities of the ISTP that you wish to acquire by using perhaps the Thomistic method of prayerful consideration, asking yourself the questions: what, why, how, when, where, who, with what helps?

The shadow qualities that the ENFJ should consider at prayer, ponder upon, and act upon are reflected in some or all of the following suggestions.

- Make a point of remembering and noticing facts and details of places, persons, events. Try to develop an eye for detail, and share this with others. Learn to give good directions to others.

- Practice logical analysis of a topic using the Thomistic prayer method.
- Make a point of being adaptable, willing to change your plans for the benefit of others.
- Keep your schedule open, unplanned, unstructured, unorganized at least one day each week.
- Be willing to be a follower doing what others want rather than always assuming the leadership.
- Be willing to live with imperfections in yourself and in others; be tolerant of your and their faults.
- Practice Franciscan prayer methods, using the beauties of nature to get in touch with the transcendental values of God and spirit.
- Practice Thomistic prayer methods to develop logical analysis and thinking.

~ The Prayer of the INFJ ~

Basic Temperament – NF
Dominant – Intuition
Auxiliary – Feeling
Inferior – Sensation
Tertiary – Thinking

Most INFJs have a strong dislike for formal prayer and repetitive prayer; however, if they have had good experiences of this type of prayer in a faith-filled community, they can use formal prayer with profit. They have a great need of silence and are attracted to centering prayer and contemplative prayer. INFJs should tithe their waking hours in order to give ten percent of their time to God and prayer; a minimum should be an hour.

For the most part, the prayer of the INFJ should be conversational prayer, just speaking to God from the heart as if to a close friend who is really present. However, a good portion of the prayer time should be given to listening and trying to discern God's will. INFJs are especially good at transposing the meaning of Sacred Scripture to today's situation. They are often good at reading the signs of the times and will often see danger ahead that is hidden from others. It is important, however, that the INFJs develop an immense trust in the goodness, love, and care of God. Since the INFJ can see problems and dangers where others remain blind, the INFJs must overcome discouragement through heroic trust in God. St. Therese of Lisieux's "Little Way of Spiritual Childhood" is especially appropriate for the INFJs.

God speaks to the INFJ especially through the Scripture. The favorite books of the Bible for this type are apt to be Isaiah (particularly chapters 40-66), Hosea, Psalms with the theme of trust and hope, the Gospels, and the Pauline Epistles. The Augustinian-type of prayer, along with the Benedictine *Lectio Divina*, will be the favorite methods of prayer. However, INFJs are usually able to adapt to personal use all types of prayer, making use of their Intuition and Feeling Functions to personalize each prayer form used.

Journal keeping may be a very effective form of prayer for the INFJs since they are usually facile in their ability to choose the right word or metaphor to express the inexpressible truths of God. Symbols and poetic images are especially important to INFJs and allow them to express their creative insights and intuitions.

INFJs, because of their spiritual vision and discernment of things hidden from others, make good counselors, spiritual directors, or soul companions. Because of the drain that such counselling and discernment makes on their inner resources, it is imperative to growth and survival that INFJs spend a good amount of time with God as well as in leisure every day to recharge their spiritual batteries. It is also important that the INFJ gets plenty of physical exercise.

The INFJs are apt to have experiences of God's love and presence which bring new, deep insights into some aspect of religion or Sacred Scripture. They may feel the presence of the Holy Spirit directing their lives and therefore should cultivate a strong devotion to the Holy Spirit in addition to a deep, personal intimacy with Jesus Christ and the Heavenly Father.

INFJs need to develop their imagination by using the Ignatian method of prayer since their shadow side is Sensing and therefore is the faculty that is the least developed in the INFJ.

Recognizing and Developing the Potential of the INFJ Shadow

Become familiar with the basic attributes of the ESTP personality, which is your opposite in type. Consider how you do not use your Inferior Function of Sensing and Tertiary Function of Thinking to the fullest. When reading the portrait of the ESTP type, what specifically struck you as so different from your customary way of acting and doing? During your period of prayer think about how these new attributes and ways of relating could be manifested in your daily living. Meditate prayerfully on each one of the qualities of the ESTP that you wish to acquire by perhaps using the Thomistic method of prayerful consideration, asking yourself the questions: what, why, how, when, where, who, with what helps?

The shadow qualities that the INFJ should consider at prayer, ponder upon, and act upon are reflected m some or all of the following suggestions.

- Develop a broader interest in other people and things.
- Be open and adaptable to others and to new events.
- Be tolerant of others, especially those with whom you disagree.
- Avoid imposing your will on others.
- Be open, listen to other people's opinions, and give them full consideration.
- Avoid hastiness in judgment and decision-making.
- Try not to overlook relevant facts and limitations. Recognize opposing factors to one's objectives and seriously consider what to do about them.
- Be alert for flaws in your own ideas.
- Develop a better eye for details, get facts straight, and try to retain them in memory.
- Practice rational and logical analysis of a situation.
- Learn to negotiate, compromise, conciliate; learn diplomacy and tact.
- Be resourceful in finding solutions to difficult situations and problems.
- Avoid being a perfectionist learning to live with imperfections and what is less than ideal.
- Take off some time without any previous planning – a day, an afternoon or evening – and just do whatever strikes you at the moment (as long as it is not sinful).
- Deliberately leave in an unorganized state some not especially-important area of your life.

- Try to enjoy whatever happens without worry, anxiety, or hurry.

~ The Prayer of the ENTP ~

Basic Temperament – NT
Dominant – Intuition
Auxiliary – Thinking
Inferior – Sensation
Tertiary – Feeling

ENTPs need challenges to bring out the best in them. Non conformists, they love to outwit the system. ENTPs are ingenious, always sensitive to new possibilities, resourceful, optimistic, enthusiastic, and are often inventors and innovators. Seldom critical, with a good sense of humor that laughs easily and often, they are gregarious.

ENTPs enjoy trying new forms of prayer, especially if they are complex. They love novelty and originality and have a strong dislike for the traditional, standardized, normal ways of doing things, even in prayer and religion, always preferring the new and fresh approach. Very resourceful, the ENTP loves the challenge of finding new ways to pray or conduct a liturgy service. However, the ENTP may become easily discouraged and lose interest when there are no new challenges.

ENTPs are best at spontaneous, improvised prayers and bored with traditional, routine prayers. Therefore, ENTPs need to discipline themselves to spend some time each day in some sort of formal prayer. The *Lectio Divina* of St. Benedict is especially appropriate. Time should be spent in spiritual reading until some new idea or insight is received. Then a substantial part of the prayer-time should be given to reflecting upon a phrase or verse of the Scripture, perhaps using it as a mantra. This is the time to be still and listen to catch any intuitions or inspirations that may come. Prayers of petition, gratitude, praise, humility, resolution, or commitment should follow. Finally, some time should be given to quiet contemplation of the new insight or truth just received.

The books of the Bible especially helpful to ENTPs are the Psalms, Wisdom, the Gospel of John, First Epistle of John, Ephesians, Colossians, and Hebrews. If the ENTP is faithful in giving quality time each day to prayer, deep and vivid experiences of the presence of God may be received.

Because of the extraverted qualities of the ENTP, a Cursillo Weekend for a new experience of Christian community is strongly recommended for this type. Prayer groups, where the practice of healing of spiritual and bodily ills is explored, may also be appealing to the ENTP.

The ENTP might benefit their spiritual life by studying the history of spirituality in order to develop a better understanding of other people's responses to, and need of, ritual, ceremony, and tradition. Contemplative prayer may come rather easily to those of this type. Since St. Teresa of Avila was likely an ENTP, her writings should be read by the ENTP; and an effort should be made to experience the different types of prayer recommended by St. Teresa. This would include intercessory prayer, reflection on the Lord's Prayer, as well as centering prayer and the prayer of quiet.

Thomistic prayer is a necessity for the ENTP. They have a great hunger and need to know and understand. Once they understand, they can usually deal with a situation.

Recognizing and Developing the Potential of the ENTP Shadow

Become familiar with the basic attributes of the ISFJ personality, which is your opposite in type. Consider how you do not use your Inferior Function of Sensing and Tertiary Function of Feeling to the fullest. When reading the portrait of the ISFJ, what specifically struck you as so different from your customary way of acting and doing? During your period of prayer think about how these new attributes and ways of relating could be manifested in your daily living. Meditate prayerfully on each one of the qualities of the ISFJ that you wish to acquire by using perhaps the Thomistic method of prayerful consideration, asking yourself the questions: what, why, how, when, where, who, with what helps?

The shadow qualities that the ENTP should consider at prayer, ponder upon, and act upon are reflected in some or all of the following suggestions.

- Be painstaking, systematic, patient with small details of some project until it is finished.
- Develop self-discipline by doing routine jobs at home or at your place of work.
- Develop and follow some routine for a whole month.
- Prepare thoroughly for some task rather than improvising as you go along.
- Be sympathetic, tactful, kind, genuinely concerned about someone in need of support.
- Be of service to someone, and minister to their every need for a week.
- Become active in social ministry working with the downtrodden, ministering to their needs and help one

of them to attain some sort of fulfillment, perhaps by finding them a new job or a new educational venture.

- Be considerate of others and of the welfare of the community.
- Follow a routine set by others in the fashion they would do it, especially in an area where you are accustomed to do things differently.
- Sacrifice your one-upmanship for a month letting others do the talking while you listen.
- Make a real effort to understand conservative people and their viewpoint.

~ The Prayer of the INTP ~

Basic Temperament – N T

Dominant – Thinking

Auxiliary – Intuition

Inferior – Feeling

Tertiary – Sensation

With great power of concentration, good memory retention, INTPs prize intelligence and may be somewhat of intellectual snobs. Having a great dislike for small talk, they quickly spot inconsistency in self or in others. This temperament is the architect, the programmer, the philosopher, the mathematician.

INTPs prefer to pray alone. In general, they need a good, logical, coherent prayer form that is in accord with truth; without it, INTPs can be turned off and abandon prayer. The INTP is able to concentrate deeply for long periods of time and needs absolute quiet and the necessary space and privacy to do so. Centering prayer should be suitable for the INTP, and a few minutes at the beginning of each day should be spent in this practice in order to center the activities of the day upon God and God's will. They absolutely need to set aside some precious time each day for quiet prayer, otherwise they will never get their act together with the Lord. Since contemplative prayer may come rather easily to the INTP, it is recommended that those of this type read the writings of St. Teresa of Avila and practice some of the prayer forms described by St. Teresa.

A variety of prayer forms can be used by the INTP. The Thomistic method of formal meditation and syllogistic reasoning will probably be the most rewarding since it uses both Thinking and Intuition. Ignatian prayer will probably be the most difficult form of prayer for the INTP because of its emphasis on sensible imagination. The INTP is often unable to use imagination in prayer or to construct vivid mental images or pictures. Attention, therefore, should be given instead to the new ideas that suddenly appear and meditation should follow on what message the Lord is giving one through these new insights.

The INTP prefers to work with impersonal ideas and thus can easily become too impersonal even with God, treating God as an object to be studied rather than a person with whom one can relate on intimate terms. The INTPs need to learn how to express their emotions and how to develop more feeling in prayer as well as in relationships with others where they tend to confine their attention to people's motives and reactions.

Probably the most valuable form of prayer for the INTP is *Lectio Divina*. After spending some time in spiritual reading, the INTP should try "listening" to God speak to one through the words just read. The INTP should practice being still to listen for any new insights, intuitions, ideas, or inspirations that may come during this quiet time. These should be carefully reflected upon to spot any inconsistency with truth. If these new ideas or inspirations seem to be in accord with truth, they should be taken seriously and steps taken to implement them. This would constitute the second phase of Lectio Divina, the Meditatio portion, and should be followed by spontaneous prayer of petition, commitment, gratitude, resolution, etc. Finally, time should also be spent in contemplation of what has occurred during the time of prayer.

INTPs should cultivate Franciscan prayer forms in order to develop their feelings and emotions. An effort also should be made to practice Augustinian prayer. Both of these will help the INTP to develop and use the Inferior Function of Feeling. INTPs state that they can get an emotional "high" from Franciscan prayer. They feel God's love for them and realize they are part of God's loving plan for the world.

Since the INTP is good at finding the correct word or words to define and describe a thing, an event, or a situation, the person of the INTP temperament is often good at composing original prayer forms to be used by others.

Recognizing and Developing the Potential of the INTP Shadow

Become familiar with the basic attributes of the ESFJ personality, which is your opposite in type. Consider how you do not use your Inferior Function of Feeling and Tertiary Function of Sensing to the fullest. When reading the portrait of the ESFJ type, what specifically struck you as so different from your customary way of acting and doing? During your period of prayer think about how these new attributes and ways of relating could be manifested in your daily living. Meditate prayerfully on each one of the qualities of the ESFJ that you wish to acquire by using perhaps the Thomistic method of prayerful consideration, asking yourself the questions: what, why, how, when, where, who, with what helps?

The shadow qualities that the INTP should consider at prayer, ponder upon, and act upon are reflected in some or all of the following suggestions.

- Try to radiate warmth and fellowship to others.
- Make a special effort to be sociable for a whole week.
- Learn to express your deepest feelings, even risk being sentimental.
- Show appreciation every day for what others do; affirm, compliment, praise.
- Attend to the needs of others and do something nice for someone each day.
- Make a point of being tactful, friendly, sympathetic with someone with whom you do not agree or toward whom you have some dislike.
- Try to bring about harmony in a situation where conflict exists.
- Make a point of noticing every detail of a room, of a scene, of a person; in other words, develop an eye for detail.
- Take time to stop and "smell the roses," using Franciscan-type of prayer.
- Be practical, realistic, matter-of-fact; use simple words and simple statements to explain something that seems obvious but is not recognized by another.

~ The Prayer of the ENTJ ~

Basic Temperament – NT
Dominant – Thinking
Auxiliary – Intuition
Inferior – Feeling
Tertiary – Sensation

The ENTJ person is known as the commandant, one who is born to lead and one who needs to lead others in order to feel fulfilled. The ENTJ seeks power and competency and is impatient with inefficiency and incompetence. Usually a very good organizer, very outgoing with people, with good intuitions, logical and rational in approach to a problem, the ENTJ wants everything planned, scheduled, structured. They enjoy working on one-, two-, or five-year plans for themselves and the organizations to which they belong.

ENTJs need good experiences of community at liturgy and prefer congregational singing to other forms of the Mass liturgy. They enjoy leading others in prayer and presiding at liturgies and prayer services. They love to be with people and not surprisingly are often attracted to charismatic prayer groups and to singing the praises of God together with others. Because the Feeling Function is the ENTJ Inferior Function, they need the help of a group or community to activate their feelings and emotions in prayer. Once activated, these feelings become a great help to their experiences of God's presence and love.

ENTJs desire a structured prayer that shows a logical, consistent development leading to a proper conclusion. The Thomistic prayer forms will probably be the most helpful type of prayer for them because of the clear structuring and emphasis on Thinking. They will find recitation of the Rosary boring but may find the Breviary or Divine Office with its structured forms of prayer helpful. ENTJs tend to be impersonal in their prayer life and need to develop their feelings and may find it difficult to pray alone. However, they need to develop regular habits of praying alone. It is strongly suggested that the ENTJ spend a few minutes at the beginning of each day using centering prayer to focus attention upon God and God's will for the events of the day.

This could be repeated occasionally during the day and again in the evening before retiring.

In addition, the ENTJ needs to set aside a regular time each day for prayer and Scripture reflection. Use of the *Lectio Divina* of St. Benedict should be profitable to the ENTJ. If the *Lectio Divina* method is used, then approximately half the time should be spent in the second part of the exercise, the Meditation and Reflection on the insight received during the spiritual reading. (The facility of the ENTJ to solve complex problems, address complex issues, and come up with creative new ideas can be put to good use during this portion of private prayer.) The Meditation should be followed by prayers of praise and gratitude, resolutions and petitions. At the end of the prayer period, the ENTJ should try to rest for a few minutes in the Lord's presence and wait quietly to see if any new thought or insight comes to mind. Quiet contemplation is needed by the workaholic, all-too-busy ENTJ, and likewise listening to uplifting music to activate spontaneous praise and gratitude and dialogue with the Holy Spirit.

Frequently the Holy Spirit will give worthwhile insights and inspirations to ENTJs during sleep. Therefore, ENTJs should try to get sufficient rest at night to experience an active dream life that can then be interpreted by their good intuitive ability. "The Lord gives to his beloved in sleep" (Psalm 127:3). The ENTJ can expect experiences of deep spiritual peace and relief from tension or pressure if a period of time is given to God in prayer each day.

Recognizing and Developing the Potential of the ENTJ Shadow

Become familiar with the basic attributes of the ISFP personality, which is your opposite in type. Consider how you do not use your Inferior Function of Feeling and Tertiary Function of Sensing to the fullest. When reading the portrait of the ISFP type, what specifically struck you as so different from your customary way of acting and doing? During your period of prayer think about how these new attributes and ways of relating could be manifested in your daily living. Meditate prayerfully on each one of the qualities of the ISFP that you wish to acquire by using perhaps the Thomistic method of prayerful consideration, asking yourself the questions: what, why, how, when, where, who, with what helps?

The shadow qualities that the ENTJ should consider at prayer, ponder upon, and act upon are reflected in some or all of the following suggestions.

- Develop your own feelings; show warmth and express feelings to others.
- Show constant appreciation for the merit and value of others. Make a point of affirming someone every day in some way.
- Be very considerate of the feelings of everyone you meet in the course of the day.
- Take time to listen to the point of view of others.
- Be open-minded, flexible, adaptable.
- Be tolerant of the mistakes, limitations, failures of others.
- Go for a walk in the woods and use the Franciscan method of prayer employing the sense impressions you perceive.
- Enjoy and practice some form of the fine arts (e.g., painting, sculpturing) just for the sake of the art.
- Without any previous planning, just take off for the day and do whatever your impulses lead you to do (as long as the actions would not be sinful).
- Develop your senses by noticing and remembering route signs and landmarks on your next car trip.

~ The Prayer of the INTJ ~

Basic Temperament – NT
Dominant – Intuition
Auxiliary – Thinking
Inferior – Sensation
Tertiary – Feeling

The INTJ is the most self-confident of all the types. Quite decisive, pragmatic, single-minded, INTJs do not like to be told what to do since they are usually fiercely independent. They are very introspective, dislike small-talk, always in a hurry, stubborn, determined. In their desire to control nature and people, they see themselves as human engineers and are usually very high achievers. They love to brainstorm for new insights, inspirations, ideas. They may appear to be cold, unemotional, reserved, and unable to express or feel emotions. Actually, their emotions are both deep and powerful. Their reluctance to express their emotions comes from fear of their inability to control them.

INTJs need much time for private prayer and are usually able to decide what is the best form of prayer for their own needs. The prayer life of the INTJ is apt to be introspective. They may be uncomfortable in public, community prayer and especially in a prayer group. A community-type retreat such as a Cursillo weekend is strongly recommended to give the INTJ person a good experience of community liturgy and celebration. The INTJ is a seeker and should experiment with as many different forms of prayer as possible to discover the type of prayer best suited to their needs. Keeping a spiritual journal may be found helpful. The Thomistic type of prayer may be the favorite. The *Lectio Divina* of St. Benedict, along with the more traditional Thomistic form of meditation, should be tried. In using *Lectio Divina* care should be taken to give equal time to Oratio and Contemplatio as to Meditatio. The Gospels, especially the Gospel of John, the Psalms, and Isaiah will probably have appeal to this type.

The INTJ needs to spend time each day in prayer and reflection. This is especially important as this type is prone to a deep inner loneliness so with quality time, the INTJ can become more God-centered and less self-centered. Such quiet time will also serve to quell anxieties about work and responsibilities. An important part of each prayer period would be quieting one's mind and trying to experience the presence of God and listening to God speak in the depths of one's heart. This takes patience, practice, and may be characterized by an absence of any noticeable benefit on many occasions. The INTJ may take the Lord's Prayer and spend half an hour saying each phrase slowly, while stopping and reflecting upon its meaning and the message each word of the phrase has. Such stillness is needed to activate the transcendent dimension of one's Intuition.

The INTJ tends to make a theoretical study of Scriptures rather than use them as a device for hearing or listening to God speak to them through text of the Bible. They must be careful not to treat God merely as an object to study in an impersonal way. Therefore, much effort should be used to develop a close personal relationship with Jesus and the Heavenly Father.

The most difficult forms of prayer for the INTJ will be the Ignatian and the Franciscan types. They should attempt these forms of prayer only when well-rested and with plenty of leisure time. They may not consider Franciscan prayer as truly prayer because of its spontaneity and informality. Their spiritual experiences are usually in the form of peaceful moments of awareness of God and the fullness of joy in the knowledge of God's love for them. Sudden answers to prayers also give them an awareness of God's presence.

Recognizing and Developing the Potential of the INTJ Shadow

Become familiar with the basic attributes of the ESFP personality, which is your opposite in type. Consider how you do not use your Inferior Function of Sensing and Tertiary Function of Feeling to the fullest. When reading the portrait of the ESFP type, what specifically struck you as so different from your customary way of acting and doing? During your period of prayer think about how these new attributes and ways of relating could be manifested in your daily living. Meditate prayerfully on each one of the qualities of the ESFP that you wish to acquire by using perhaps the Thomistic method of prayerful consideration, asking yourself the questions: what, why, how, when, where, who, with what helps?

The shadow qualities that the INTJ should consider at prayer, ponder upon, and act upon are reflected in some or all of the following suggestions.

Develop an eye for detail, and look for the transcendental qualities of sensible realities.

- Listen frequently to good music, with your eyes closed; do nothing else but just enjoy the music and experience the beauty therein.
- Learn to work better with others by being open to the different ways of other temperaments.
- Be patient and tolerant with those who disagree with you.

208

- Develop some close friendships which require a good deal of your time and energy.
- Be generous in sharing what you have with others—generous to a fault; give without expecting anything in return.
- Show respect for someone in authority even though you do not like that person.
- Try to resolve some observable conflict among others in the community.
- Be willing to revise your ideas, opinions, plans.
- Take time to "smell the roses" and enjoy life.
- Occasionally act on impulse.
- Be willing to waste time, seemingly doing nothing but engaging in small talk or useless conversation.

Summary Guidance Based on Dominant, Auxiliary, Tertiary, and Inferior Functions

The ISFJ and ESFP Types

Dominant – Sensation

Activate the transcendent dimension of the Sensing Function through Franciscan-style prayer to gain deeper insights into the intangible realities of God.

Watch filling up time with sensible activities and ignore deeper, spiritual realities.

Auxiliary – Feeling

Be open to the voice of the Holy Spirit speaking within the depths of the conscience, especially when in conflict to discern which will do the most good and the least harm to everyone concerned.

Take seriously any new insights that spontaneously come to mind, striving to combine them with traditional teachings in order to form an authentic conscience.

Inferior – Intuition

Seek unifying symbols that show harmony and balance in own life and in the events of history. These living symbols will be recognized when they result in a profound and moving inner experience or feeling of joy, peace, love, and hope.

Tertiary – Thinking

Set aside weekly time for the Thomistic method of prayer to look for new insights and flashes of grace particularly to get a better grasp of some complex issue.

The ISFP and ESFJ Types

Dominant – Feeling

Activate the transcendent dimension of the Feeling Function embracing love, awe, reverence, joy, fear, respect toward God through Ignatian, Augustinian, and Franciscan types of prayer.

Watch maintaining a proper balance in personal feelings toward God by listening as well as speaking.

Auxiliary – Sensation

Form appropriate sense images of God and all that belongs to God such as any beautiful or awe-inspiring experience of nature.

Nurture comparisons, analogies, parables, and figures of speech, which, in turn, will become living symbols offering a deep, emotion-filled experience of God's presence and loving care.

Inferior – Thinking

Realize capability to simplify a complex problem or issue by cutting through external details and discerning the underlying unity that is present.

Search for some living symbol or comparison which will give a new insight into spiritual realities.

Tertiary – Intuition

Set aside weekly time for the Thomistic method of prayer, looking for new insights concerning God, a relationship with Him, relationships with others, and the proper relationship between the conscious ego and the unconscious inner-self.

The ISTP and ESTJ Types

Dominant – Thinking

Activate the transcendent dimension of the Thinking Function through Thomistic-type prayers, along with *Lectio Divina*.

Watch turning prayer into an intellectual exercise or approaching with robotic steps.

Auxiliary – Sensation

Experience the presence of God, power of God, love and goodness of God in all creation.

Look for any images that may be pregnant with deeper meaning and for unifying symbols or ideas or images that bring together opposing ideas.

Inferior – Feeling

Seek out an authentic, God-centered prayer group or community and be fully engage in the feelings and values of the group.

Be willing to express feelings in front of others (for example, tears of joy and sorrow) to overcome a cold-fish, ice-in-veins, detached attitude.

Tertiary – Intuition

Set aside weekly time for the Augustinian method of prayer being patient to catch the occasional intuitions, inspirations, insights that rise to the surface of consciousness.

The ISTJ and ESTP Types

Dominant – Sensation

Activate the transcendent dimension of the Sensing Function through Ignatian prayer to find new insights of the intangible realities of God's wisdom, power, and love.

Watch falling into hypocrisy by following an external code of morality which is contrary to deepest convictions.

Auxiliary – Thinking

Seek to connect the traditional doctrines of the Church and teachings of Scripture.

Rely upon discernment if conflicts arise between personal convictions and traditional doctrine.

Inferior – Intuition

Be alert to symbols and images that express the harmony, unity, and balance of the whole of reality.

Reflect on any images, analogies, comparisons, and figures of speech that may spontaneously come to your attention or through reading or other activities.

Tertiary – Feeling

Set aside weekly time for the Augustinian method of prayer particularly personalizing verses of the Bible which can act as a direct message from God and greatly enrich your understanding and prayer life.

The INFJ and ENFP Types

Dominant – Intuition

Activate the transcendent dimension of the Intuition Function through Augustinian prayer being open to new insights that arise from the unconscious about God.

Watch the tendency to abandon liturgy or prayer when it is predictable or rote.

Auxiliary – Feeling

Form strong personal relationships with a God-centered prayer group or community to share spiritual growth and practices.

Keep Jesus as the focal point of prayer to form a deep and intimate relationship of love.

Inferior – Sensation

Cultivate an appreciation of beauty, art forms, dance, music, drama, fiction to discover appropriate images, comparisons, analogies, symbols to express spiritual realities.

Tertiary – Thinking

Set aside weekly time for the Ignatian method of prayer as a means to opening a doorway to new images concerning spiritual realities and relationships.

The INFP and ENFJ Types

Dominant – Feeling

Activate the transcendent dimension of the Feeling Function through Augustinian prayer to energize and open a deep, beautiful intimacy with God.

Watch being prescribed, or choosing, a single, static method of prayer which will diminish experience of God's presence.

Auxiliary – Intuition

Seek and find unique, personal methods of prayer to connect with God and to experience His presence.

Be open to guiding others in finding appropriate ways of prayer.

Inferior – Thinking

Reflect on God's wisdom, power, goodness, love, and promises of mercy and forgiveness to deepen trust in God's loving care and providence.

Tertiary – Sensation

Set aside weekly time for the Thomistic method of prayer, having patience to perceive the underlying unity of the diverse spiritual realities and cut through complex situations.

The INTJ and ENTP Types

Dominant – Intuition

Activate the transcendent dimension of the Intuition Function through Thomistic prayer by creatively uniting past, traditional knowledge with new, living symbols of God and spirituality.

Watch making prayer life more a study than a real encounter with the living God as He exists today.

Auxiliary – Thinking

Focus on individual scripture passages taking time to "draw some fruit and benefit," as St. Ignatius says, from each contemplation.

Allow time to indulge in lengthy abstract thinking about God and spiritual realities

Inferior – Sensation

Cultivate an appreciation of beauty, art forms, dance, music, drama, fiction to discover appropriate images, comparisons, analogies, symbols to express spiritual realities.

Tertiary – Feeling

Set aside weekly time for the Franciscan method of prayer to reach wholeness and balance and to attain deep intimacy with God.

The INTP and ENTJ Types

Dominant - Thinking

Activate the transcendent dimension of the Thinking Function through Thomistic prayer to develop a sense of awe, reverence, joy, love, peace as a result of the new insights into Truth.

Watch for over-structuring, or over-planning, prayer time to control the experience and limit spontaneity.

Auxiliary - Intuition

Be open to catching the insights, inspirations, and intuitions that suddenly occur in the course of daily activities as well as during the time of formal prayer.

Seek interpretation of dream symbols and other images, not repressing them but finding authentic meaning.

Inferior - Feeling

Seek good group experiences of prayer, e.g., good community liturgies, prayer groups, to share in the feelings and values of others in order to deepen experiences of God and divine grace.

Allow the emotions connected with love to surface consciously and be acknowledged in front of at least one other trustworthy person.

Tertiary - Sensation

Set aside weekly time for the Franciscan method of prayer using the imagination to develop suitable images, analogies, comparisons with spiritual realities and thus connect with God and spiritual realities.

CHAPTER TEN

TEMPERAMENT &
LITURGICAL PRAYER

When considering God and the things of God, we are dealing
with inexpressible, numinous realities that are transcendental to
the physical world in which we live. We have no literal way of
describing these spiritual realities and so we are forced to rely on
metaphor, comparison, analogy, or images which we call symbols.
Therefore, any relationship with God on earth will necessarily
involve the use of symbols, which are the sensible means by which
the transcendentals express themselves in our conscious life.[1]
Jesus constantly used symbolic language in his attempts to tell
us about God and our relationship with God. Some examples of
the symbols used by Jesus in his teaching would be calling God
"Abba" or "Daddy" or using metaphors like "kingdom of God,"
"heavenly banquet," "sower and seed," "mustard seed," "treasure
hidden in a field." The parables of Jesus are extended symbols of
God and our relationship with God. Symbols can be audible (the
words of Sacred Scripture), visible (the community of believers

at a Eucharistic celebration), tangible (the crucifix), tasteful (the bread and wine of the Eucharist), or olfactory (the smell of burning incense).

In addition to individual symbols we also use a series of symbolic events to express the process of our becoming united with the life of God and to explain the practice of our religious beliefs. We call this a myth.[2] Through ritual or liturgy, a myth is told again and again in order to bring the life of the community into harmony with the life of God. The best-known Christian myth is the Paschal Mystery which relives the progression of life, death, and resurrection. The Eucharist is the ritual which we use to relive and make real this Paschal Mystery. By repeating the story of the Paschal Mystery again and again, the community of believers becomes a part of the process of death to the old and resurrection to a new and more transcendental level of life.

A myth becomes alive, active, effective, and productive of new grace and new psychic energy through the collective, living symbols which are activated in the minds and hearts of those listening to or participating in it. The main purpose of public liturgical services is to make these collective symbols come alive. When a congregation comes together to relive the myths of their religious history, the symbols and rituals used in the liturgy must be effective and real so that the present members can become a part of the history of salvation and thus make the myth a part of their lives.

Authentic religious symbols can be either dead or alive, depending upon whether or not the symbol is able to move minds, wills, feelings, and lives. For a great many Christians today, the symbols used in the liturgy are no longer living symbols and thus no longer affect or change their lives. There is a big difference between a dogma of faith in which we believe and a living symbol of the faith which we experience. Dogma is a rational attempt to describe the object of our faith, while a living symbol gives us an experience of God. Symbols put life into the dogmas of faith so that they become real and meaningful. Because different human temperaments apprehend symbols in a different way, depending upon which function is Dominant and Inferior, a knowledge of temperaments will greatly aid in the task of restoring life to our religious symbols and our liturgies.

The Symbols of the Eucharist

The Holy Eucharist was instituted by Jesus Christ to give Christians the opportunity to be united with God on earth just as Jesus was united with his Heavenly Father during his life on earth. For Christians the Eucharist is the principal way to establish and maintain this contact with Jesus and, through Christ, with God during the in-between times marking the interval between the first coming of Jesus to earth and his final coming. This Eucharistic union with the Risen Lord is accomplished by means of four living symbols: Community, Word, Cross, and Meal. These four symbols respond to the four psychological functions of Feeling (Community), Thinking (Word), Sensing (Cross), and Intuition (Meal). To experience the presence of the risen Lord through these four symbols, the transcendent dimension of each of the functions must be activated. Otherwise, the particular symbol that corresponds to that function will remain lifeless and useless to the participants in the liturgy.

The four symbols also respond somewhat to the spiritual needs of the four basic human temperaments. The experience of community appeals especially to the SP (Franciscan) temperament.

The Word of God excites the interest of the NT (Thomistic) temperament with its search for truth. The vivid reliving of the Cross fascinates the historically-conscious SJ (Ignatian) temperament. The eschatological dimensions of the ritual meal challenge the future-oriented NF (Augustinian) temperament. A well-conducted Eucharistic liturgy thus presents four different ways for the congregation to experience the presence of the Risen Jesus. (1) We celebrate the real presence of Jesus through the coming together of the community of believers. "Where there are two or three gathered together in my name, there I am in the midst of them," as Jesus says in Matthew 18:20. (2) We contemplate the Word of God from the Sacred Scriptures. St. Augustine says that when we proclaim the Word of God in the Eucharist we are just as much in the presence of the Holy Spirit as we are in union with Christ when we partake of the Eucharistic bread. (3) We commemorate the Paschal Mystery of the Cross. "Every time you eat this bread and drink this cup you proclaim the death of the Lord until He comes" (I Cor 11:26). (4) We anticipate the heavenly banquet of eternity through the ritual meal of Holy Communion.

If the Eucharist is to be an effective instrument in bringing about and maintaining an earthly union between the Lord and ourselves, these four major symbols of the Mass must be living symbols and not mere lifeless signs. Symbols become alive whenever the transcendent dimension of the corresponding functions is activated. The more fully we can activate this transcendent dimension, the more alive, meaningful, and grace-filled the Eucharistic celebration will be. Because different temperaments find it easier to activate the transcendent dimension of one function rather than another, a good Eucharistic celebration should endeavor to evoke the use of all four functions through the four basic symbols of the Eucharist. Otherwise, some persons in the congregation will not be reached and affected. A knowledge of human temperaments and some insight into the different ways to activate the transcendent dimension of each of the four psychological functions will help to accomplish this.

As the Eucharist is now constituted, the main burden for a good experience of the presence of the Risen Lord falls upon the priest or celebrant. The celebrant's task, therefore, is to see that the Eucharistic celebration, and especially the homily, satisfy the different spiritual needs of the four basic temperaments. The celebrant must be aware that different human temperaments are affected in different ways. For instance, a logically developed homily will resonant with those whose Dominant is Thinking. If delivery is pleasant and well-modulated, the Sensors will take notice more readily, and likewise, if tone and body langue convey sincerity and enthusiasm, the Feelers and the Intuitives will respond. Furthermore, if theological concepts are presented, the NTs will be satisfied; while a hearkening back to tradition and the history of doctrinal development will alert the SJs to attention and interest. If comment is made on how the readings relate to one's life today, the NFs will be reached; whereas, if a dramatic action of self-denial or mission is called for, the SPs will emotionally and mentally respond.

With the emphasis of Vatican II on the ministry of lay persons and the formation of liturgy committees in parishes, more people can, and should, be taught how to assist the presider in making the liturgy a drama that will sweep one's being up into a fuller participation in the life of the Risen Lord. In any good theatrical or play production, preparation and adherence to detail must be done beforehand to set the stage properly. For the ritual of the Mass, the cast and crew (the laity) can help the director of the liturgy (the priest-celebrant) by creating a correct and beautiful setting (altar appointments, flowers, lighting, acoustics, and sound) and by being prepared for participation by previous study of the Word to be proclaimed. In preparation, also, in the form of advance notice and reviews, a liturgy committee can work to arouse a feeling of community so that when all congregate, the warmness of the group leads to the anticipation of a "good show," namely, a fine Christian celebration of the Eucharist. Thus, all functions and temperaments, represented in the congregation, will be involved; and they in turn will assure that the liturgy speaks to the other persons of the same temperament in the congregation.

The Feeling Function and the Community of Believers

The basic symbol present at the Eucharist is the community of baptized persons who accept Jesus Christ as their Lord and Savior and who believe in the power of his life, death, and resurrection to save them. Without a congregation of believers constituted of a celebrant or leader and at least one or more persons, it is impossible to have a complete Eucharist. An ancient law of the Church specifies that a priest should not celebrate the Eucharist alone but only with a congregation. In the Gospel Jesus says, "Where there are two or more gathered in my name, there I am in the midst" (Matt 18:20). Belief in the presence of the Risen Lord in every gathering of Christian believers is an elemental symbol of Christianity that goes back to the first Pentecost.

The Feeling Function, which grasps the value of personhood, must operate in order to have an experience of community. The transcendent dimension of the Feeling Function must be activated in order for a Eucharistic congregation to experience and accept the presence of the living, Risen Lord in their spirit-filled community. Feeling or emotion is not sufficient to experience the real presence of Jesus Christ. Faith, which has made a value judgment, and grace, which is God's gift, must also be present; but faith and grace without the transcendent dimension of the relational Feeling Function will not engender community.

Without a well-activated transcendent dimension of the Feeling Function, which relates to God as a person and to the presence of Christ in each believer, the symbol of community in Christ and in one another becomes a dead symbol. Hence, the necessity on the part of the celebrant, ministers, and congregation to prepare for the liturgy beforehand by developing an intimacy with the Lord during their personal prayer periods throughout the week. If everyone has worked hard to develop a relationship with Jesus Christ Our Lord during their daily personal prayer-time, the Eucharistic celebration will resound with the intense feeling of the assembled and become a tremendous experience of the presence of God. Through prior preparation, the sense of the presence of the Lord and a sense of community become very real and powerful during the Eucharistic celebrations of a vibrant retreat group or any other group which has shared in study and preparation. Even though the persons on retreat have previously been strangers to one another and are observing strict silence, a beautiful community experience nevertheless may be had each time the group gathers for Eucharist; and in that community celebration together they have a new and tremendous experience of the presence of the Lord Jesus Christ among them.

The key word to describe this experience of community is *celebration*. Wherever a group of spirit-filled Christians gather for

Eucharist, a celebration of our oneness in faith occurs in that we all have heard and believe in the Good News of Jesus Christ. Even Christian funeral masses are a celebration – not of death but of our faith in resurrection. All the four basic temperaments and all sixteen personality types need and can enjoy the experience of a community celebration. Because the NF temperament usually has the most highly developed Feeling Function and understands best the value of personhood and community, the NF persons in the congregation have a special responsibility to see that this symbol of community remains alive and active, rather than lifeless and useless, during each liturgy. The SJ persons who have Feeling as either their Dominant or Auxiliary Function will be a great help to the NFs toward making the symbol of community alive and vibrant. Whereas, those SJ persons, whose Feeling Function is their Inferior or Tertiary Function, are like the NTs who need a community celebration in order to activate their dormant Feeling. Probably the SP persons need the experience of community most; so much so that, if this dimension of Eucharist is absent, the SPs soon vote with their feet and stop attending the Eucharist gathering.

Before Vatican II, a great deal of the power of the Eucharistic symbol of community was lost. For most Catholics, the Mass was a private encounter with God and many had developed their own individual ways of connecting with God at Mass. Those who had succeeded best were the most upset with the liturgical reforms. Instead of allowing their private devotions to continue during Mass, the Church insisted that they experience the reality of a Christian community. Since the reforms of Vatican II, we have had varying success in restoring new life to the Eucharistic symbol of community. There is still much resistance to it from many quarters and much work still to be done to make this symbol a living experience of the presence of the risen Lord Jesus Christ.

We are suggesting here that one of the best ways to make this symbol of community a living symbol is the activation of the transcendent dimension of the Feeling Function, which should begin with the celebrant, include all those who assist in the Eucharistic celebration, and then reach out and embrace the whole congregation. However, to wait until Sunday morning to start activating one's Feeling Function is to wait too late. All week long during a daily prayer period the priest, ministers, and congregation need to concentrate on attaining an intimacy with God and a relational attitude toward others by bringing their Feeling Function into conscious expression.

The Thinking Function and the Word of God

After community, the next most obvious symbol present in the Eucharist is the comprehension of the Word of God in the Sacred Scriptures. Almost immediately after the community gathers for liturgy, the reading or proclamation of the Word takes place. Every word of the Sacred Scriptures is a symbol of the presence and power of God and God's truth upon earth; and when properly explained and understood, these words become a true experience of His living presence. Although the lectors and homilist have the primary responsibility to "break open" the Word of God so that it becomes fully intelligible to the assembled, the proclamation of the Word of God at liturgy requires the cooperation of everyone in the congregation. Each member of the community has a responsibility not only to listen attentively and intelligently but also to prepare for the liturgical proclamation of the Word by previous study of the Scriptures at home. Any member of the congregation who approaches the liturgical proclamation of the Word without prior preparation is doing a disservice not only to themselves but also to the rest of the congregation.

The conscious use of the Thinking Function, as well as the activation of the transcendent dimension of the Thinking Function, are needed in order to make the Word of God alive and meaningful. The conscious dimension of the Thinking Function is activated through the study of Scripture commentaries, Bible history, and the other available source knowledge of the Bible; but the transcendent dimension of Thinking will open the door to the transcendental level of truth where God dwells and thus lead to a deeper, inner spiritual wisdom.

The Bible is called the Word of God because it is more than mere human words. It is a message from the transcendent God. Human words by their very nature are finite and limited, whereas God is infinite and unlimited. When God communicates with human beings, He adjusts Himself to our level and uses human language and terms. These human words of the Bible have a richer meaning than the obvious, literal, human sense. We need therefore to activate the transcendent dimension of our Thinking Function in order to interpret authentically the true meaning of God's Word. We speak of the need "to break open" the Scriptures in order to discern their deeper, spiritual meaning. To accomplish this, we need a combination of divine grace, faith, knowledge, and understanding through the activation of the transcendent dimension of all four functions but especially through that of Thinking and Intuition.

Therefore, it would be natural to expect that those with the NT temperament should make the greatest contribution to instilling new life into this second Eucharistic symbol, the Word. Actually, all the temperaments and all the functions have a part to play if the proclamation of the Word of God during the Eucharist is to become truly vibrant and speak to each member of the Christian community. St. Paul speaks of the Word of God as a two-edged sword which is able to convict, convince, convert, and sanctify. If the symbol of the Word is truly alive, abundant evidence of its power will be seen in a visible experience of conversion and metanoia on the part of the congregation. In the history of Christianity, we have had many experiences when the symbol of the Word was truly alive and converted thousands of persons: for instance, through John and Samuel Wesley in England, St. Francis Xavier in India, Jonathan Edwards in this country, St. Francis of Assisi in Italy.

The Eucharistic symbol of the Word is present not only during the proclamation at the Liturgy of the Sacred Scriptures, but also in all the other words used throughout the Eucharistic celebration including the songs that are sung. All of us have experienced how grace-filled and meaningful a Eucharist can be when there is good and appropriate singing in which the congregation can participate. Also, our Catholic and Christian faith postulates that the words of the Eucharistic Prayer, especially the Words of Institution, when spoken with faith, have the power to make really and truly present the living Lord Jesus under the appearances of the bread and wine.

The key word to describe our reaction to the living symbol of the Word is *contemplation* of divine Truth. Whenever the symbolism of the Word is truly alive, the whole Eucharistic congregation will find themselves "lost" in contemplation of the power and presence of the truth of the living God.

The Sensing Function and the Cross

From the very beginning of Christianity, the Eucharist has been seen as proclaiming the Paschal Mystery of the death of Jesus on the cross. St. Paul, writing to the Corinthians a mere 20 or 30 years after the events of Good Friday, stated "Every time you eat this bread and drink this cup, you proclaim the death of the Lord until he comes" (I Cor 11:26). Catholic theology has defined the Mass as "the unbloody sacrifice of the Cross." In the Gospels, Jesus uses the symbol of the Cross to express the path of non-violence which he chose to follow and which he insisted his disciples also follow. All the functions have a part to play to make and keep the symbol of the Cross a living force in the Eucharist.

We need to think about the true meaning of the cross, and we need to activate our Feeling Function in order to identify with the sufferings of Jesus on the cross. Our Intuition will also help us understand the hidden Mystery of the Cross. However, the Sensing Function will be the most affected when we reflect deeply upon this symbol of the Cross and the Crucifixion. The outward sufferings connected with the crucifixion are meant to symbolize a whole new way of life introduced by Jesus Christ to resolve the problem of evil in the world. Sensors, who live in the present, in the here and now, are the types who are most prepared to incorporate this dimension of the Christ-life into their own life. Therefore, we all need to activate the transcendent dimension of our Sensing Function in order to appreciate the spiritual value of the Cross.

The symbol of the Cross is closely connected to another ancient symbol which is still very much present in the dreams of modern people as well as in the mythology of ancient peoples. Throughout history the symbol of the dragon has been used to express the powers of evil confronting mankind on earth. In the third chapter of Genesis, the forces of evil are represented by the serpent, which is but another, more devious, form of the ancient dragon.

The long-recommended method for the handling of a dragon was to slay it; and we see a similar attitude toward evil throughout most of the pages of the Old Testament. The violence of evil was met by the violence of the sword, and thereby the power of evil was counteracted or neutralized for the time being. The most dramatic example of this method of handling the dragon of evil was the fierceness employed by Joshua and the Israelites when they entered Canaan. However, this method of "slaying the dragon" never proved to be permanently effective in eliminating evil and establishing peace. Invariably the dragon revived in the next generation and continued its opposition to good; and a new wave of violence was undertaken to neutralize the power of evil once again. This has been the constant experience of the human race in its struggles with the powers of evil on earth.

By his passion and death, through the paradox of the cross, Jesus instituted a new way of conquering the dragon. In the goodness of his love, Jesus submitted himself to the dragon and allowed it to kill him. To all outward appearances the forces of evil conquered Jesus on Good Friday. The "dragon" seemed to have won an uncontested victory over the forces of good by putting the God-man to death. However, God's last word was not spoken on Good Friday but on Easter Sunday. The last word was not death on a cross but the new, glorious, immortal life of the Risen Lord. Thus, the symbol of the Cross was introduced into human history as God's ultimate answer for resolving the problem of evil on earth. Victimhood was presented to the world as the way of lasting peace. A new chapter was written in the ancient epic of the conquering of evil.

This new way of encountering and conquering the dragon was so revolutionary, so different from the traditional way of handling one's enemies and confronting evil, that only the first few generations of Christians really took it seriously. In the first 300 years Christian martyrs did practice victimhood, and the result was the "conquest" of paganism in both the West and the East. However, beginning with Constantine in the fourth century and continuing through the Middle Ages and modern times, we once again resorted to the pagan method of attempting to slay the dragon. Christians revived this ancient pagan myth in the legend of St. George and the dragon; and during the centuries of Christian knighthood the cross became a sword for slaying the enemies of Christianity. Holy wars were fought in the name of God and Jesus Christ; and theologians, beginning with St. Augustine, devised the conditions for conducting a *just* war. Most Christians soon took it for granted that the use of violence was justified in overcoming evil when all other methods failed. It became the patriotic duty of Christians to take up the sword in defense of their country and its rights.

The Cross was still mounted on church steeples and other religious buildings; and the Mass was still spoken of as the unbloody sacrifice of the cross; but for all practical purposes, and for most Christians, after the fourth century, the Cross lost its symbolic meaning as God's way for handling the dragon of evil in the world. We still spoke of "taking up our cross and following Christ," but we used the symbol of the Cross merely to mean the sufferings, struggle, and pain which individual humans had to experience on earth in order to lead a good and Christ-like life.

The symbolism of the Cross did not die out completely, but the meaning given to it by Jesus was greatly emasculated.

Amazingly, a non-Christian, Mahatma Gandhi, rediscovered the full symbolism of the Cross and re-introduced Jesus's teaching on victimhood into the modern world. The non-violent methods for overcoming evil practiced by Gandhi contain all the elements of authentic Christian victimhood. Martin Luther King, Jr. also used non-violence to vanquish the evil of racism in this country. Now, in the face of the terrible threat of a world-wide nuclear holocaust, victimhood is again being suggested as the Christian solution to a lasting world peace. Instead of trying to slay the dragon, we are challenged to convert the dragon by love, truth, goodness, and non-violence even at the price of our own death. We seem to have rediscovered the symbolism of the Cross as taught and practiced by Jesus on Calvary.

On the night before he died, Jesus gave to the Christian community a means, the Eucharist, to relive and proclaim the symbol of the Cross in every succeeding generation. If this third symbol can become alive and meaningful in our Eucharistic liturgies, we today would thereby receive the necessary grace, strength, and courage to take up our own cross and victimhood and follow this Christian way of conquering the dragon. However, for this to happen, the transcendent dimension of the four psychological functions needs to be activated and experienced during the Eucharist. We must look beyond the mere, outward, sensing appearances of Jesus's crucifixion and see the Cross as a symbol of agapeic love whereby we, here and now, can overcome the evil of the world. By our Feeling Function we will activate the power to love our enemies as Jesus did and respect their dignity. We must activate the transcendent level of our Thinking Function to perceive the Cross as the reconciling symbol of truth which resolves the problem of evil. Through our Intuitive Function we can see the problem of evil from the expanded viewpoint of God rather than through our own human keyhole vision.

The key word to describe this third symbol, the Cross, is commemoration. More than a mere pious remembrance of Jesus's death, liturgical commemoration means "making present" once again the past event in order for the people of today to become a part of the never-ending experience of the Paschal Mystery of the Cross. An authentic celebration of the Eucharistic Liturgy enables us to experience anew the victimhood of Jesus on Calvary; and if this third symbol, the Cross, is truly alive, the participants in the liturgy receive the grace and psychic energy to offer themselves, after the example of Jesus, as victims of love to counteract the powers of evil in the world. The SJ persons in the congregation should be the first to understand, appreciate, and preserve this dimension of *commemoration*. Therefore, they have the main responsibility to help those of other temperaments experience the true meaning of the liturgical commemoration of the Cross. However, all the functions and all the temperaments have a contribution to make if we are to restore full life to the Eucharistic symbol of the Cross.

The Intuitive Function and the Ritual Meal

The fourth symbol of an authentic Eucharistic liturgy is the ritual meal which is meant to be an anticipation of the heavenly banquet to which we are invited after death. The first Eucharist celebrated by Jesus the night before he died was a ritual meal which we call the Lord's Supper. In using a ritual meal, Jesus followed the Jewish traditions which used the context of a sacred meal to express God's presence, friendship, and union with the chosen people. The first of these, the Passover Supper, celebrating God's continual protection and presence among them, has been a religious symbol for more than three thousand years. Jesus would have also adhered giving a blessing both before and following a meal (see Deut. 8:10). In these blessings, the head of the house recalled the whole history of God's salvation of His people making the God of their ancestors really and truly present.

Similarly, most Christians have believed from the very beginning that the Eucharistic meal made the Risen Lord Jesus really and truly present to them. The first Christian communities acknowledged that the ritual meal of the Lord's Supper was actually a Christian Passover meal whereby believers in Christ could celebrate their delivery from the Angel of Death just as the Israelites were delivered in Egypt through the Passover.

Therefore, a ritual meal of commemoration became the relational symbol through which the living presence of the Risen Lord was experienced at the gatherings of the early Christians. We are told that on the first Easter Sunday evening the two disciples at Emmaus recognized Jesus in the breaking of the bread. Down through the centuries the majority of Christians have continued to believe in the real presence of the Risen Christ under the appearances of the bread and wine at the Eucharistic meal. Unfortunately, much of the symbolism of a sacred banquet in our Eucharistic celebrations has been lost. A stranger would find it difficult to recognize the average Sunday Liturgy as a sacred banquet or meal. The only survival of this symbol of eating and drinking is at Holy Communion where more often than not the eating consists of a thin, round, white wafer placed on the tongue or in the hand of the communicant and may, or may not, have access to the cup. Even the most vivid and creative imagination has difficulty seeing this state of affairs as a heavenly banquet.

When Jesus instituted the Eucharist at the Last Supper he speaks of this ritual meal as an anticipation of everlasting life: "He who eats my flesh and drinks my blood has everlasting life and I will raise him up at the last day. For my flesh is food indeed and my blood is drink indeed" (Jn 6:54-55). Intuition, which is the future-looking faculty of the human psyche, is needed to appreciate this dimension of *anticipation* in the Eucharist. The Eucharistic meal is meant to be a foreshadowing of our eternal union with God and the Risen Lord Jesus in heaven. Just as the communion bread and wine of the Eucharist are incorporated within us when we eat and drink them, so intuitively, and symbolically, we should experience here now on earth through the Eucharistic meal something of that future heavenly union with Jesus. "The cup of blessing which we bless, is it not a participation in the blood of Christ? The bread which we break, is it not a participation in the body of Christ?" (I Cor 10:16).

By activating the transcendent dimension of the Intuitive function, we should be able to experience each Eucharist as a return of the Risen Lord to earth to refresh and strengthen us with the food and drink of his own resurrected body and blood. Through divine grace and faith, the transcendent dimension of our Intuition grasps and accepts this. We are able to see each Eucharist as an experience similar to that described in the last chapter of St. John's Gospel where the Risen Lord returns to earth at the Sea of Tiberias. After directing the apostles where to cast their nets, he invites them to bring their boats ashore and serves them a meal of fish and bread. During the Liturgy of the Word, the Risen Lord returns to our midst in order to instruct us where "to cast our nets for a catch." Then, in the ritual meal of bread and wine, Jesus refreshes and strengthens us for our journey in faith toward the kingdom of heaven. Through grace-filled Intuition we can have an experience of anticipation of the heavenly banquet of the future kingdom.

Thanks to the liturgical reforms of Vatican II we once again are able to experience the living symbols of Community and Word. Also, our new understanding and acceptance of "victimhood" can bring new meaning to the symbol of the Cross. But, ways must be found to put new life into the symbol of the sacred meal. Besides Intuition, the other three functions – Sensing, Thinking, and Feeling – must be activated in their transcendent dimension to restore life to the nearly dead symbol of a ritual meal.

Since 75 percent of the average congregation have Sensing as their Dominant or Auxiliary Function, the first appeal should be to arouse the transcendent dimension of Sensing. For example, we can make more obvious the symbolism of the breaking of the bread before Holy Communion. Large hosts or larger loaves of Eucharistic bread might be used; and then these should be broken in full view of the congregation with a verbal recollection of St. Paul's statement to the Corinthians to vivify the communal meal aspect. "Because the loaf of bread is one, we, many though we are, are one body, for we all partake of the one loaf" (I Cor 10:17). Furthermore, people should be urged to partake sufficiently of the cup of consecrated wine rather than merely touching the cup to their lips. A pleasant-tasting wine should be chosen and an adequate quantity taken so that its sweetness and tingling warmth will be felt by the communicant. "Taste and see the sweetness (goodness) of the Lord."

The homilist at the Mass can activate the symbol-making dimension of the Thinking Function of members of the congregation by explaining the implications and tradition of a community meal. Once this is pointed out, everyone can recognize the symbolic meaning of sitting down to a meal with friends. To sit down at table and eat with another human being is universally recognized as a sign of friendship and an acceptance of our tablemates as equals. As a ritual meal, the Eucharist very clearly expresses the willingness and desire of Jesus Christ to be our friend and tablemate. Just as the Risen Christ ate and drank with his apostles after the resurrection, so he continues to accept us as his friends at the Eucharistic table. He invites us to his table, and through the act of partaking in Holy Communion we are assured of a place at his heavenly banquet in heaven.

The Thinking Function also allows one to reflect upon the symbolism of the many grains of wheat crushed to be ground into flour and submitted to the oven's heat to be baked. We, though many members, also need to be ground into flour and baked in order to become the Body of Christ. As the many small grapes which are crushed and fermented to become the wine, we too must experience diminishment and suffering to join ourselves to our fellow human beings in order to become the one body of Christ.

During Eucharist the Feeling Function may also be activated in regard to the symbol of a meal by recalling a similar ritual which is used the world over to express hospitality. When a guest visits, the host is usually expected to offer something to drink and perhaps something to eat. This offering by the host and the acceptance by the guest is universally recognized as a symbol of hospitality and friendship. One would not make such an offer to someone, or accept it from someone, whom one considered an enemy. Furthermore, when a reconciliation is achieved between two former antagonists, the universal symbol to express this is by the two persons having a cup of coffee together, or having a drink together, or in some way sharing food and drink together. Similarly, the Eucharistic meal, with its partaking of the bread and cup, is a symbolic act which expresses God's love and friendship for us and our acceptance of this love and our reciprocation of friendship toward God. It is also meant to be a symbolic act expressing our intention to practice love and friendship toward our neighbor.

To What Purpose

The fact that down through the centuries the Eucharist has continued to be a source of grace and a means of sanctification for countless persons is proof enough that the power of its symbols never has been lost completely. *Community, Word, Cross,* and *Meal* are always present in every valid celebration of Eucharist. However, a great deal of grace and psychic energy have been lost by the failure of modern persons to appreciate fully the meaning of these four symbols. The rediscovery of the power of symbols by modern depth psychology and the subsequent interest in them should help to revitalize our Eucharistic symbols.[3]

Each of the four psychological functions and each of the four temperaments have a distinct contribution to make to modern liturgical renewal. The more proficient we can become in using the transcendent dimension of each of the functions during our personal prayer, the more we will be able to contribute to making the Sunday Liturgy a true experience of the presence and power of the living God and the Risen Lord Jesus Christ. Together, the four symbols of Community, Word, Cross, and Ritual Meal can give us an experience of unity with God, with the Risen Jesus, and with the whole Communion of Saints, both living and dead.

CHAPTER ELEVEN

CONCLUDING THOUGHTS:
THE FOUR R's OF LECTIO DIVINA

Although this book advocates different methods of prayer, *Lectio Divina* stands as the basic format for a daily period of formal prayer or meditation for everyone. The other four methods described in this book are specific variations of *Lectio Divina*. Ignatian, Augustinian, Thomistic, and Franciscan prayer differ from one another primarily in the second step of *Lectio Divina*.

By following the four steps of *Lectio Divina*, we open our psyche to God's presence through our four functions: Sensing, Thinking, Feeling, and Intuition. An easy way to remember the four steps of *Lectio Divina* is to think of them as the four R's: Reading (*Lectio*), Reflecting (*Meditatio*), Responding (*Oratio*), and Resting (*Contemplatio*). In Reading, we use our Sensing function to get some new insights into God's revelation in the Bible or some other religious book; we also can "read" the manifestation of God in all reality. In Reflecting, we use our Thinking function, our rationality or intellect, to make an application of the Word of God to our life today. In Responding, we use our Feeling function to respond with love to God's word or call. In Resting, we allow God to use our Intuitive function to suggest new insights concerning God and God's relation ship with us. Through the transcendent dimension of the four functions God becomes present to us through the symbols of the revealed Biblical words. The four steps of *Lectio Divina* form a good check-list to assure that we have used all four functions during our daily prayer period.

Ignatian Prayer

In this prayer method, at the *Meditatio* or Reflection, by using our sensible imagination we project ourselves back into the original historical event described in the Bible. We try to make the event that happened two or three thousand years ago become alive. We think of God's marvelous deeds of the past. In the process of remembering or commemorating these Biblical events or words, we make God present to work similar marvelous deeds for us. Thus, we are able to experience some of the same graces and blessings as did those persons who were historically present for the original event recorded in the Bible. We use this method especially during the course of celebrating the church's liturgical year.

Augustinian Prayer

In this prayer-method, during the second step, Reflecting (*Meditatio*), we use our Thinking function to transpose the Scriptural words and events to our present situation. Thus, by creative imagination we try to make the Biblical words become meaningful to us today. We imagine God once again speaking the words of the Bible, but this time it is to us personally in our present situation. Since God and Jesus are the same, yesterday, today, and forever (Heb. 13:8), we can expect that God will show us the same love and faithfulness as was shown to the persons and in the events described in the Bible.

Thomistic Prayer

By analysis of the Biblical text during the Reflection period, the Thomistic approach helps us to make a practical application of the words of Scripture. The transcendent dimension of the Thinking function is used to discern God's will for us: for instance, what the next step for our growth and development might be. The purpose of such reflection and analysis of God's words is to attain an intellectual conviction regarding some virtue we will now try to practice or some fault we will try to avoid. Through our reflection, we attempt to reach a resolution of our problems logically in the light of Christian teaching.

Franciscan Prayer

During the second step of *Lectio Divina*, Reflecting (*Meditatio*), Franciscan prayer uses the transcendent dimension of the Thinking function in order to make God become alive and real in the present-day experiences of our life. By reflecting upon how the characters in the Bible experienced God in the events of their lives, we realize God's presence and actions in our own. We rejoice and celebrate God's many gifts to us and respond with the consecration of ourselves to God and God's will. Our meditation becomes inspiration and aspiration. Brother Lawrence in his little book, *The Practice of the Presence of God*, gives an excellent example of Franciscan prayer.

Dangers of Single-Focus

We are firmly convinced from our experience in working with hundreds of different people that the suggestions given in this book will strike a responsive chord. Try them, use them for a while, experiment with the different types of prayer until you discover for yourself the type, or types, of prayer best suited to you. However, when you find that one style, do not allow yourself to become stifled with just one type of prayer. There is, in fact, a danger in exclusively following any one type of prayer.

Ignatian spirituality must be on its guard against Phariseeism or Externalism which was so thoroughly condemned by Jesus in the Gospels: "These people honor me with their lips but their hearts are far from me" (Matt 15:8).

For Franciscan spirituality, the heresy of "good works" or Pelagianism is the extreme against which one must be on guard. The free spirit must practice self-discipline and spend some formal time with God each day. Otherwise, good works will degenerate into mere secularistic humanism, the prevailing religion of the majority of Americans today.

Augustinian spirituality must beware of the heresy of Manicheanism, to which Augustine himself fell victim. We may become so engrossed in the things of the spirit that we begin to neglect the body and to think of the things of the flesh as evil, losing sight of our creation and that "God saw everything that He had made and behold it was very good" (Gen 1:31).

Thomistic spirituality is apt to be a very intense form of spirituality and can fall victim to Jansenism which grossly exaggerates the requirements needed for salvation, thus denying heaven to a major portion of the general population. Religion and prayer then become an elitist movement which is only for those who follow all the obligations which the NT architects of sanctity dream up in their speculations. We know that Jansenism among Catholics and Puritanism among Protestants have done great harm to the religious life of our people. There is always this danger of carrying something good to the extreme of fanaticism, thus making it no longer totally beneficial but potentially harmful.

Even *Lectio Divina*, if used without being balanced by virtual prayer of action, could result in too much introspection.

Conclusion

As stated in the Introduction, everything said in this book about the relationship of temperament and prayer should be taken with certain reservations. Our recommendations will not necessarily resonate with everyone since each of us is a unique person with our own particular background of experience. However, since so many people have benefited from the suggestions found herein, the authors feel justified in presenting their findings and conclusions to a wider audience. Moreover, the great interest aroused by our Prayer Project of 1982 indicated the need of assembling under one cover the various papers we have written.

Our hope is that this book will stir up even more interest in the subject so that many others will proceed along this thesis and make further contributions to it. The hunger and thirst for more knowledge concerning spirituality, prayer, and their relationship to personality type and psychological functioning can be satisfied only if many others apply their wisdom and experience to the subject.

Enjoy the riches of all the different kinds of prayer by, making the effort to practice those forms of prayer which require extra psychic energy and effort on your part. Your pains will be rewarded.

USING THIS BOOK
ON RETREAT

One-Day Retreat Outline

A one-day retreat introduces the Temperaments and gives individuals time to consider the different prayer types and what may personally resonate.

Opening Prayer/Meditation

What We Hope to Achieve

- Determine / confirm our Temperament – The MBTI can be administered during the retreat (such as the night before a full-day); if that timing does not work, it is best that participants know their Type beforehand
- Review Temperament and its effects on Christian Spirituality
- Understand the Prayer Types associated with the Temperaments
    - Review each Temperament and its Prayer Type
    - Spend individual time in prayer using each method suggested by the book

The Four Spiritualities – An Overview

- Augustinian Spirituality
- Franciscan Spirituality
- Thomistic Spirituality
- Ignatian Spirituality

Benedictine Prayer – *Lectio Divina*

- Overview
- The Four Steps
  - Lectio
  - Meditatio
  - Oratio
  - Contemplatio
- Break off for individual time practicing and journaling using one of the *Lectio Divina* prayer suggestions from Chapter Three

Ignatian Prayer and Spirituality (SJ Temperament)

- SJs make up 46 percent of population
- Review characteristics of SJ Temperament
  - Pride themselves on being dependable, helpful, and hard-working
  - Loyal mates, responsible parents, and stabilizing leaders
  - Tend to be dutiful, cautious, humble, and focused on credentials and traditions
  - Concerned citizens who trust authority, join groups, seek security, prize gratitude, and dream of meting out justice
- Review Ignatian Prayer
  - Commemoration

- Projection
- Sensible imagination
- Ten steps in Ignatian Prayer
- Break off for individual time practicing and journaling using one of the Ignatian Prayer suggestions from Chapter Four

Augustinian Prayer and Spirituality (NF Temperament)

- NFs make up 10-15 percent of population
- Review characteristics of NF Temperament
    - Enthusiastic, trust their intuition, seek their true self, prize meaningful relationships, and dream of attaining wisdom
    - Pride themselves on being loving, kindhearted, and authentic
    - Giving, trusting, spiritual, and they are focused on personal journeys and human potentials
    - Inspirational leaders
- Review Augustinian Prayer
    - Transposition
    - Creative imagination
- Break off for individual time practicing and journaling using one of the Augustinian Prayer suggestions from Chapter Five

Franciscan Prayer and Spirituality (SP Temperament)

- SPs make up about 30 percent of population
- Review characteristics of SP Temperament
    - Tend to be fun-loving, optimistic, realistic, and focused on the here and now
    - Pride themselves on being unconventional, bold, and spontaneous
    - Troubleshooting leaders

- Excitable, trust their impulses, want to make a splash, seek stimulation, prize freedom
- Review Franciscan Prayer
  - Full use of the five senses
  - Spirit-filled prayer
  - God in the whole of Creation
- Break off for individual time practicing and journaling using one of the Franciscan Prayer suggestions from Chapter Six

Thomistic Prayer and Spirituality (NT Temperament)

- NTs make up 10 percent of population
- Review Characteristics of NT Temperament
  - Pragmatic, skeptical, self-contained, and focused on problem solving and system analysis
  - Pride themselves on being ingenious, independent, and strong willed
  - Strategic leaders
  - Even-tempered, they trust logic, yearn for achievement, seek knowledge, prize technology, and dream of understanding how the world works
- Review Thomistic Prayer
  - Scholastic Method of Thinking
  - Orderly progression of thought from cause to effect
  - What, Why, How, Who, Where, When, with What helps?
- Break off for individual time practicing and journaling using one of the Thomistic Prayer suggestions from Chapter Seven

Summary and Conclusion

Closing Prayer/Meditation

Two-Day Retreat Outline

A two-day retreat provides opportunity to get more specific into the individual MBTI Types as well as explain the Shadow and Inferior Function in prayer.

Opening Prayer/Meditation

What We Hope to Achieve

- Determine / confirm our Temperament – The MBTI can be administered during the retreat (such as the night before a full-day); if that timing does not work, it is best that participants know their Type beforehand
- Review Temperament and its effects on Christian Spirituality
- Understand the Prayer Types associated with the Temperaments
- Review each Temperament and its Prayer Type
- Spend individual time in prayer using each method suggested by the book (end of day one)
- Review of best prayer options for the sixteen individual types
- How to use our Shadow and Inferior Function in Prayer

(Follow the above outline for the first day of the retreat and then continue on the second day as below)

Confirming Our Temperament

- Group individuals according to their Preference (SF, NF, ST, NT).
- Have them create responses to what they like about themselves, what they dislike/would like to change, what

they wish others knew about them, what animal or song or image best captures them.

- Regather the full group together for each Preference to present.

Prayer Suggestions for the Sixteen Individual Types

- Break off for individual prayer and journaling using prayer recommended for that type. Include instruction to have each person write one to three words that capture their approach to prayer or what they feel they want as their priority when praying.
- Reassemble and discuss how this experience may have differed from trying all of the different methods the previous day and have each person share their words.

The Transcendent Dimension of the Four Functions

- Review the ability of Sensation, Intuition, Thinking, and Feeling to connect with the spiritual levels of reality.
  - Discerning the Inferior and Tertiary Functions
  - How to activate the Transcendent Dimension of the Four Functions
- Match individuals up who have the same Dominant, Auxiliary, Tertiary, and Inferior Functions: ISFJ and ESFP; ISFP and ESFJ, ISTP and ESTJ, ISTJ and ESTP, INFJ and ENFP, INFP and ENFJ, INTJ and ENTP, INTP and ENTJ. (It may be that you do not have all sixteen types in your retreat group; if that is the case, be sure to keep the same Preferences together, e.g., SF, NT, etc.) Have the groups talk through their Functions and develop plans particularly for ways to activate the transcendent dimensions (see end of Chapter Seven and

discussion of each Function in Chapter Nine).

- Reassemble and ask for volunteers to discuss a few lessons learned.

Using Our Shadow Function in Prayer

- Seeking wholeness, we bring about a relationship between the Ego, the Shadow, and God.

- Match individuals up with their shadow type: the ESTP and INFJ, ISTP and ENFJ, ESTJ and INFP, ISTJ and ENFP, ESFP and INTJ, ISFP and ENTJ, ESFJ and INTP, and ISFJ and ENTP. (It may be that you do not have all sixteen types in your retreat group; if that is the case, an alternative way to group would be by Preferences: NF with ST and NT with SF.) Have the groups discuss what each of their customary way of acting and doing and how it differs from the other type (see Chapter Seven for prompts).

- Reassemble and ask for volunteers to discuss a few lessons learned.

Summary and Conclusion

Closing Prayer/Meditation

APPENDIX II

THE 1982 PRAYER PROJECT

As discussed in the Introduction, the Prayer Project was launched in 1982. After learning about the Myers-Briggs Type Indicator (MBTI), and using it in retreats and with individuals in spiritual direction, we decided to determine if we could establish a connection between MBTI and prayer. To recruit participants, we asked for volunteers from the 800 individuals who were on our mailing list for The Open Door bulletin, which was a regular, mailed communication in pamphlet form. From that request, 415 responded, agreeing to help us discern the value of various prayer forms for the different psychological types of human personality.

Each individual took, or had taken, the MBTI, the Keirsey-Bates Temperament Sorter, or the Gray-Wheelwright Jungian Type Survey to determine their type prior to participating. Consequently, we knew that our participants represented all sixteen of the individual types. Throughout the year-long project, regular reports of their reactions to the different prayer suggestions and other material, which we sent them, were returned to us.

From their responses, we were able to ascertain that 98 percent (407 participants) found value in choosing a method of prayer compatible to their temperament. Of the 2 percent (8 participants) who said that they did not find the suggestions that helpful, based on their returned questionnaire, we determined that they experienced a unique state of prayer and contemplation empowered by the Holy Spirit.

With the help of the feedback and suggestions given by the participants, we corrected any inaccuracies that had existed in our theories concerning the relationship between temperament and particular forms of prayer, which are reflected in this publication.

Participants
Total Number: 415
Men: 155 (27.7%)
Women: 300 (72.3%)

Affiliation
Clergy: 44 (10.6%)
Women Religious: 84 (20.2%)
Lay Persons: 287 (69.2%)

Types and Temperaments

SJ = 133 participants = 32%
- ISTJ   21
- ESTJ   16
- ISFJ   65
- ESFJ   31

SP = 43 participants = 10.4%
- ISTP   9
- ESTP   3
- ISFP   24
- ESFP   7

NT = 44 participants = 10.6%
- INTJ   18
- INTP   7
- ENTP   8
- ENTJ   11

NF = 195 participants = 47%
- INFJ   53
- INFP   56
- ENFP   50
- ENFJ   36

ENDNOTES

Notation is made of the original sources used by the authors, some of which may now be out of print or republished with newer editions. These sources were included as a separate bibliography; therefore, in some instances, the connection of the source to the text is an estimate and some sources would have been used more extensively throughout the writing. In this edition, updates for online resources and more recent research are included as applicable.

Introduction to the 30th Anniversary Edition

[1] Arguments over the reliability of the MBTI are longstanding. Academics tend to be the harshest critics; see, for example, Adam Grant, an organizational psychologist at the University of Pennsylvania's Wharton' School, who has written a couple of blog posts on the topic including this one in which he also explains his preference for the Big Five: https://www.linkedin.com/pulse/20130922141533-69244073-mbti-if-you-want-me-back-you-need-to-change-too.

Supporters can be found across the spectrum mostly from practitioners such as this blog by a dating agency that uses both MBTI and the Big Five with its clients (see https://boo.dating/blog/is-the-mbti-legitimate) and from some peer-reviewed journal articles (see, for example, Carlson, John G. "Affirmative: In Support of Researching the Myers-Briggs Type Indicator." *Journal of Counseling & Development*, vol. 67, no. 8, Apr. 1989, p. 484). There is also a text from the MBTI publisher: Lawrence, Gordan and Martin, Charles. *Building People, Building Programs: A Practitioner's Guide for Introducing the MBTI® to Individuals and Organizations*. Gainesville, FL: Center for Application of Psychological Type, 2001.

As a point of clarification, the MBTI was founded on identifying *preferences* in relation to cognitive functions and is thus not an indicator of *personality* type, like the Big Five. Please note that the authors of this book use the terms "preferences" and "personality" interchangeably.

2 Goldbrunner, Josef. *Holiness is Wholeness and Other Essays.* Notre Dame, IN: University of Notre Dame Press, 1964. (out of print)

3 Exclusive interview with Chester P. Michael. Slow Reads: Reading for Ruminants. https://slowreads.com/2011/04/24/exclusive-interview-with-chester-p-michael/

Introduction

1 The authors relied upon the following two publications:

Myers, Isabel Briggs. *The Myers-Briggs Type Indicator 1962 Manual.* Palo Alto, California, Consulting Psychologists Press, 1962.

Myers, Isabel Briggs. *Introduction to Type.* Palo Alto, California: Consulting Psychologists Press, 1980.

If you have not taken the MBTI, you are encouraged to do so before reading this book. There are hundreds of online resources for taking a self-assessment and finding descriptions of each of the sixteen individual types; the instrument can be found at MBTIonline.com and type characteristics at themyersbriggs.com. There are other versions of the MBTI, or MBTI type instruments, but their statistical validity and reliability are not established, and they are not supported by the voluminous research associated with the MBTI.

2 Keirsey, David and Bates, Marilyn. *Please Understand Me: An Essay on Temperament Styles.* Del Mar, California: Prometheus

Nemesis Books, 1978, pp. 5-11.

Keirsey distinguishes four temperaments, or personality types, which are referred to throughout the book. "Temperament" is the characteristic or habitual inclination of a person to choose one attitude or one function rather than another as their customary behavior. The book includes a self-test; it can also be found online by searching for the Keirsey-Bates Temperament Sorter. In addition, at keirsey.com, there are trait assessments specifically for professional development.

3   The Gray-Wheelwright Jungian Type Survey can be found online.

4   "Type" refers to the group or category of individuals who have common qualities of personality that serve to distinguish and identify them. In this book we use the word "type" when talking about the sixteen different Jungian types as determined by the MBTI, according to the dominant attitudes and functions. Type is distinguished from "trait," which occurs along a spectrum. The MBTI has been criticized for failing to include the degree of its personality characteristics, but such criticism is misplaced because traits are not what classic MBTI theory describes.

5   One text which the authors examined was Bryant, Christopher. *Prayer and Different Types of People*. Gainesville, Florida: Center for Application of Psychological Type, 1983.

6   Goldbrunner, Josef. *Holiness is Wholeness and Other Essays*.

Chapter One—An Overview of the History and Development of the Theory of Temperament

1   Jung's findings were published in English in 1923. In

writing this book, the authors relied upon the volume: Jung, Carl Gustav. *Psychological Types.* Princeton: Princeton University Press, 1976.

2   Myers, Isabel Briggs with Myers, Peter. *Gifts Differing.* Palo Alto, California: Consulting Psychologists Press, 1980.

3   Keirsey & Bates, *Please Understand Me.*

4   To determine to which of the four basic temperaments (NT, NF, SP, SJ) you belong, take the second letter of your four-letter personality type, which will be either an S or an N. If it is an S, then take the fourth letter of your personality, which will be either a J or a P. Thus, you will have two letters, either SJ or SP. If your second letter is an N, take the third letter of your personality type, which will be either a T or an F. Again, you will have two letters, either NF or NT. These then constitute the four basic temperaments: SJ (Ignatian), SP (Franciscan), NT (Thomistic), and NF (Augustinian).

5   The functions are identified as Dominant, Auxiliary, or Secondary, Tertiary, or Third, and Inferior, or Fourth. The Dominant function is the one which is most developed, and easiest to use, and therefore is the preferred way one operates in conscious life. The Secondary function is also relatively conscious and is often employed in support of the Dominant function. The Tertiary function is less conscious than the Secondary, and often operates as a bridge between conscious and unconscious life. As such, it can serve as a gateway to the life of the spirit. The Inferior, or Fourth, is the function which is the least developed and least used. Because it requires the most psychic energy when used, we tend to avoid inferior functions particularly if tired or preoccupied. Always the opposite of the conscious Dominant Function, the Inferior Function, as determined by the MBTI, will be the Dominant Function of one's unconscious since the unconscious is the opposite of one's consciousness. The

authors referred to Schemel, George J. and Borbely, James A. *Facing Your Type*. Wernersville, Pennsylvania: Typrofile Press, 1982, which is now out of print.

6 The unconscious is that vast area of the human psyche (personality, soul, spirit) which is beyond the grasp of our conscious faculties. The unconscious, according to Jungian theory, is divided into the personal unconscious of forgotten or repressed memories of one's past life and the collective unconscious which contains the heritage of images and memories of the whole human race. A more modern understanding for the collective unconscious is the behavioral predispositions that are transmitted genetically, primarily via psychic imagery.

7 "Shadow" refers to all of those elements of the psyche of which we are presently unconscious. At times Jung used "shadow" and "unconscious" as synonyms for the same reality. We have both a positive and negative shadow. The positive shadow is the vast potential for good which is waiting to be activated into conscious life and subjected to our conscious will. The negative shadow is the totality of all those faults and evil tendencies in our nature of which we are presently unaware but which nevertheless influence our life.

8 Psychic energy is all of the power and energy available to a person from one's inner being as well as from one's conscious spiritual faculties. Psychic energy is often used as the psychological synonym for divine grace. It is a grace when used constructively in conscious life; but since it is raw, undifferentiated in the unconscious, it can also be used destructively for evil purposes if one should so choose.

9 Keirsey & Bates, *Please Understand Me*, 30-66.

10 In the first edition, the authors were of the opinion that one's Myers-Briggs type could change over the course of a lifetime. This is no longer the predominant view among Depth Psychologists or experts in the field of the MBTI. According to the MBTI Manual: "Type theory assumes that type does not change over the lifespan. Rather, the expression of type may vary in accordance with different stages of life and different life circumstances." To learn more, see Myers, Isabel Briggs, McCaulley, Mary H., Quenk, Naomi L., and Hammer, Allen L. *MBTI Manual: A Guide to the Development and Use of the Myers-Briggs Type Indicator* (3d Ed.). Palo Alto, Consulting Psychology Press, Inc., 1998, 28.

11 Von Franz, Marie-Louise and Hillman, James. *Lectures on Jung's Typology* (2d Ed.). Thompson, Connecticut: Spring Publications, 1998.

12 Grant, W. Harold, Thompson, Magdala and Clarke, Thomas E. *From Image to Likeness: A Jungian Path in the Gospel Journey.* Ramsey, New Jersey: Paulist Press, 1983.

13 Sanford, John A. *The Kingdom Within.* Philadelphia: J. B. Lippincott, 1970. Sanford draws on the work of Carl Jung and does not include the MBTI.

Chapter Two—How Temperament Affects Christian Spirituality

1 Sanford, *The Kingdome Within,* 16-25.

2 For a more complete examination of the Christian spiritual tradition see Lane, George, S. J. *Christian Spirituality: A Historical Sketch.* Chicago: Loyola Press, 1984.

3 Known in Latin as *Sub Tuum Praesidium,* this is the oldest known prayer to the Virgin Mary. It was discovered in a Greek papyrus, c. 300 A.D., and later translated to Latin.

For more, see https://ssvmusa.org/index.php/2016/01/10/
sub-tuum-praesidium-an-ancient-prayer-to-mary-during-
times-of-persecution/

[4] The authors' reference is Pennington, M. Basil. *Centering Prayer: Renewing an Ancient Christian Prayer Form.* Garden City, New York: Doubleday and Co., 1980. There are many other books that explain the history and practice of centering prayer including those by Fr. Thomas Keating, Cynthia Bourgeault, and David Frenette. Consider *The Path of Centering Prayer: Deeping your Experience of God* by Frenette with a foreward by Father Keating (2012, Boulder, Colorado: Sounds True).

The Cloud of Unknowing, written in the fourteenth century by an unknown author, forms a primary basis for the mystical journey including the practice of Centering Prayer.

[5] See Bacovcin, Helen, trans., *The Way of a Pilgrim.* New York: Doubleday, 1978. This book, written by an unknown nineteenth-century Russian peasant, tells stories related to the power of the simple Jesus Prayer. (The extension of *The Pilgrim Continues His Way* contains references to the anti-Semitism prejudice sadly prevalent against the Russian Jew on the eve of the pogroms, which were large-scale, targeted anti-Jewish rioting.)

[6] For more on the Jesus Prayer, Centering prayer, and Lectio Divina, see Konkler, Paul, O.C.S.O. *Don't You Belong to Me? A Basic Introduction to the Spiritual Life.* Ramsey, New Jersey: Paulist Press, 1979.

[7] Dating to 397, the Rule of Augustine is the oldest monastic rule in the Western Church. To learn more, see *Augustine's Rule: Introduction and Commentary* by Adolar Zumkeller (1987). Also see Augustine, Saint. *The Confessions of St. Augustine,* translated by John K. Ryan. Garden City, New York: Doubleday Image Book, 1960.

8 In our Prayer Project, 48 percent of those participating were NFs. We have also seen NFs as the majority in the retreat movement such as Cursillo. Cursillo is short for *Cursillo de Christianadod*, "a little course in Christianity," an apostolic movement developed in Spain in 1944 and popular in many U.S. Catholic dioceses as well as Episcopal, Lutheran, and other Christian churches. The Cursillo experience is an excellent instrument for developing a properly balanced emotional involvement in religion. For more information, see cursillo.org or natl-cursillo.org.

9 Hutchinson, Gloria. *Six Ways to Pray from Six Great Saints.* Cincinnati: St. Anthony Messenger Press, 1982.

10 See *The Little Flowers of Saint Francis of Assisi* by Brother Ugolino, particularly Part I, Chapter 8, in which St. Francis explains what things are perfect joy.

11 à Kempis, Thomas. *The Imitation of Christ*, translated by Ronald Knox. San Francisco: Ignatius Press, 1959. Book One, #3, 25.

12 The authors drew upon two specific sources for Ignatian prayer (1) Fleming, David J., S. J. *Modern Spiritual Exercises.* Garden City, New York: Doubleday Image Books, 1983. (2) Puhl, Louis J. *The Spiritual Exercises of St. Ignatius.* Chicago: Loyola University Press, 1951. In addition, also see de Mello, Anthony, S.J. *Sadhana: A Way to God*. St. Louis: The Institute of Jesuit Sources, 1979, which draws primarily upon the Ignatian method of prayer.

13 Liturgical prayer is the official public prayer of a community of believers. For Catholics, this is primarily the Eucharist. It also includes the other Sacraments and public prayers of the Church, such as the Divine Office, the Blessing of Palms or Ashes, the Christian Wake, etc.

¹⁴ Teresa of Avila, Saint. *Interior Castle*, translated by E. Allison Peers. Garden City, New York: Doubleday Image Books, 1961.

¹⁵ See also Teresa of Avila, Saint. *The Way of Perfection*, translated by E. Allison Peers, Garden City, New York: Doubleday Image Books, 1964.

Welch, John, O.C. *Spiritual Pilgrims: Carl Jung and Teresa of Avila*. Ramsey, New Jersey: Paulist Press, 1982.

Chapter Three—Benedictine Prayer Lectio Divina

¹ A reconciling symbol is an image rising out of the unconscious which succeeds in bringing together and uniting two apparently opposite values or truths.

² Meier, John. *Matthew*. Collegeville, Minnesota: Michael Glazier Series Liturgical Press, 1980.

Chapter Four—Ignatian Prayer and Spirituality: The SJ Temperament

¹ Sensible imagination is the faculty of the soul that enables us to form in our mind images of present and past sensory experiences. (For example, we can imagine some scene from childhood or the face of a distant relative or friend.) It is the normal way most people think, and it is done without abstract reasoning.

² Keirsey & Bates, *Please Understand Me*, 39-47.

³ The authors' original suggestion of 40 percent of the population being SJ falls in the low-end of current metrics. The Myers & Briggs Foundation offers the frequency of each type based on compiled results from 1972–2002; for SJ, the frequency is 46 percent of the population   (see https://

www.myersbriggs.org/my-mbti-personality-type/my-mbti-results/how-frequent-is-my-type.htm). Keirsey refers to SJs as "guardians" who constitute 40 to 45 percent of the population (see https://keirsey.com/temperament/guardian-overview/).

4   In vocal prayer, we actually speak the words of the prayer. Vocal prayer may be recited aloud or whispered or merely formed with one's lips. In vocal prayer, we usually use the words of someone else rather than our own spontaneously formed words. The Rosary is a typical example of vocal prayer, although it is also intended as meditative or contemplative prayer by reflection upon one or another of the mysteries of the life of Jesus Christ and Mary.

5   Like prayer, when it comes to learning, what works for one person will not necessarily work for another. See Lawrence, Gordon. *People Types and Tiger Stripes: A Practical Guide to Learning Styles.* Gainesville, Florida: Center for Application of Psychological Type, 1979.

Chapter Five—Augustinian Prayer and Spirituality: The NF Temperament

1   Creative imagination is the facility to create new images and symbols that will express some spiritual truth which otherwise could not be clearly understood. Primarily the work of the Intuitive Function, one's creative imagination works best when all four psychological functions are working at a transcendent level. The parables and images used by Jesus are examples of the creative imagination at work striving to explain the mysteries of God.

2   Keirsey & Bates, *Please Understand Me*, 57-66.

3   The Myers & Briggs Foundation gives the NF number as 10 percent of the population (see https://www.

myersbriggs.org/my-mbti-personality-type/my-mbti-results/how-frequent-is-my-type.htm). Keirsey groups NFs as "idealists" who comprise 15 percent of the population (see https://keirsey.com/temperament/idealist-overview/).

4   The "self" is the ordering and unifying point of the psyche around which coalesces the totality of the unconscious inner being. In a mature person, the "self" becomes the central director of one's entire life, both the unconscious and conscious. For believers, it is the image of God, implanted at the center of our inner being, according to which our whole nature is directed. It is the point of our inner being and personality that is most closely in touch with God and the Holy Spirit and from which we receive the divine energies of grace.

5   The authors use the term "symbol" as an image which attempts to express some aspect of the spiritual dimensions of reality. Carl Jung defined "symbol" as an attempt to express the inexpressible.

6   The first edition did not list liberal/conservative; the text read: "…Communists ?????" [sic]. The change was made in this edition to achieve a similar sentiment, and emphasis upon, a labeled "enemy."

Chapter Six—Franciscan Prayer and Spirituality: The SP Temperament

1   The Myers & Briggs Foundation gives the SP number at 27 percent of the population (see https://www.myersbriggs.org/my-mbti-personality-type/my-mbti-results/how-frequent-is-my-type.htm). Keirsey groups SPs as "artisans" who comprise 30 percent of the population (see https://keirsey.com/temperament/idealist-overview/).

2   Keirsey & Bates, *Please Understand Me*, 30-39.

3 Virtual prayer is prayer of action, whereby we express our love, faith, and devotion to God primarily by actions of loving service toward our fellow human beings. The emphasis is upon purity of intention, i.e., keeping the thought and will of God constantly in the forefront of our mind as we go about doing the work of the Lord and serving the needs of our brethren.

4 Charismatic prayer consists primarily of prayers of praise and gratitude to God. It often includes praying in tongues and prayers of prophecy and healing. The emphasis is upon "praying in the Spirit," which refers to putting oneself completely in the hands of the Holy Spirit, and allowing the Spirit to use our tongues and bodies and minds.

Chapter Seven—Thomistic Prayer and Spirituality: The NT Temperament

1 The Myers & Briggs Foundation gives the NT number at 10 percent of the population (see https://www.myersbriggs.org/my-mbti-personality-type/my-mbti-results/how-frequent-is-my-type.htm). Keirsey groups NTs as "rationals" who comprise 10 percent of the population (see https://keirsey.com/temperament/rational-overview/).

2 Keirsey & Bates, *Please Understand Me*, 47-57.

3 Metanoia is a Greek word used by New Testament writers to describe the change of direction in one's life required by the Gospel teachings of Jesus. A synonym for "metanoia" would be "conversion." It is sometimes translated as *repentance*, *reform*, or *to do penance*.

4 Thérèse of Lisieux, Saint. *The Story of a Soul*. Washington: Institute of Carmelite Studies, 1972. See particularly chapter ten.

Chapter Eight—Using Our Shadow and Inferior Function in Prayer

1 Keirsey & Bates, *Please Understand Me,* 188.

2 Chapter Nine will explore using the Shadow further. For additional reading, see Chapter 11, "Our Shadow Always Follows Us," in *Arise: A Christian Psychology of Love* by Michael, Chester P. and Norrisey, Marie C. Charlottesville, Virginia: The Open Door, Inc., 1981.

3 *Numinous* is used in this book as an experience of being filled with the presence of divinity or the Holy (as contrasted with the physical or material) dimensions of reality.

4 Psychological functions are the four ways by which we perceive and judge reality: Sensation and Intuition (the two perceiving functions) and Thinking and Feeling (the two judging functions). The MBTI measures the relative strength of conscious orientation and adaptation of each of these four functions. In each person they are developed to varying degrees and in various combinations and are modified by one's attitude of either extraversion or introversion.

5 This classification of the extraversion or introversion of the tertiary function represents what the authors have come to believe based upon their experience in counseling and spiritual direction. However, *The MBTI Manual, Third Edition,* states that the tertiary function will be the same as the auxiliary function. We write based on our observations that for introverts the dominant and tertiary functions will be introverted, while only the auxiliary and the fourth (inferior) functions will be extraverted. For extraverts, the opposite applies; i.e., the dominant and tertiary functions will be extraverted, while the auxiliary and the fourth (inferior) functions will be introverted.

6   Whitmont, Edward. *The Symbolic Quest.* Princeton: Princeton University Press, 1969.

7   von Franz, Marie-Louise & Hillman, James. *Lectures on Jung's Typology.* Irving, Texas: Spring Publications, Inc., 1979.

8   When we speak about ego, we are referring to the "I" of one's life, the focal point of consciousness around which cluster all the conscious faculties. It is the center of one's conscious life as contrasted with the Self which is the focal point of one's unconscious being. The ego has the responsibility for directing our conscious life. To do a good job of this, the ego needs to be in contact with the inner Self and maintain a balanced tension with the Self. In a mature person the Self will be the true center of both conscious and unconscious life.

9   Conscious faculties refer to the intellect, will, imagination, memory, feeling, five bodily senses, or all those powers or abilities of which one is conscious and can use consciously.

10   Active imagination is a method of assimilating unconscious contents (dreams, fantasies, etc.) through some form of self-expression as a process of freeing up the unconscious from control of the ego. For a more thorough explanation, see von Franz & Hillman, *Lectures on Jung's Typology.*

11   Assagioli, Roberto. *Psychosynthesis.* New York: Viking Press, 1971. In ISP, certain symbolic motifs are presented to the one who seeks to come in contact with the depths and heights of their own spiritual potential by activating the transcendent dimension of one of the functions. Other names given to this method of activating the transcendent dimension of the four functions are Jung's active imagination, Mary Watkins' waking dreams, and

Robert Desoille's directed daydream. ISP, or any of these, can be effectively used in spiritual direction.

[12] King, Martin Luther, Jr. *Letter from Birmingham Jail.* Penguin Modern. London, England: Penguin Classics, 2018.

Chapter Nine—Prayer Suggestions for the Sixteen MBTI Individual Types

[1] As discussed, there are several online resources for discovering your type and for reading about each type's characteristics including on myersbriggs.org; a web search will yield many different resources. In addition, in Keirsey & Bates *Please Understand Me,* there is an appendix on the 16 types and information can be found on the website keirsey.com.

[2] Lawrence of the Resurrection, Brother. *The Practice of the Presence of God,* translated by John J. Delaney. Garden City, New York: Doubleday Image Books, 1977. See also the classical text from the fourteenth century, written in Middle English by an unknown author, which tackles the mystical approach to God. Johnston, William, trans. *The Cloud of Unknowing.* William Johnston. Garden City, New York: Doubleday Image Books, 1973.

[3] Intercessory prayer is prayer of petition where we ask God to grant us some favor. For some people this is practically the only form of prayer that they use. The authors believe that praise, gratitude, and contrition – as well as meditation, contemplation, and reflection on God and the truths of God – should also be a part of one's prayer life.

Chapter Ten – Temperament and Liturgical Prayer

[1] Assagioli, *Psychosynthesis*, 287-303.

2 A myth is a story, often enacted in ritual, which expresses in symbolic language a religious or philosophical idea and evokes a response from one's inner being. A myth may or may not be literally true. Either way, the myth sets forth a profound truth that transcends the literal meaning." Unfortunately, many people think a myth is a mere legend, existing only in the imagination and without objective reality. According to Webster's Dictionary this is a secondary meaning for myth and is not the meaning we are using here. For more, see Kelsey, Morton. *Myth, History, and Faith: The Remythologizing of Christianity.* New York: Paulist Press, 1974.

3 See particularly Jung, Carl Gustav. *Psyche and Symbol,* "Transformation Symbols in the Mass." Garden City, New York: Doubleday Anchor Books, 1958. 148-224. Remember that in Jungian psychology the personality as a whole is called the psyche, which is the Greek word for soul or spirit. Therefore, the psyche includes both the conscious faculties and the totality of our unconscious life.

The authors also referenced Jacobi, Jolande. *Complex, Archetype, Symbol: In the Psychology of C. G. Jung.* Princeton: Princeton University Press, 1959.

About the Authors

Monsignor Chester P. Michael, a Roman Catholic priest ordained in 1942, devoted a substantial part of his priestly ministry to spiritual direction, preached retreats, and workshops on prayer and spirituality. A student of Jungian psychology since studies at Notre Dame University in the 1950s, he received a Doctorate in Sacred Theology in 1975 from St. Mary's University in Baltimore. He is the author of six books and wrote and published a quarterly bulletin, "The Open Door," addressing spirituality, theology, scripture, and psychology. Msgr. Michael died in 2014; his work continues via the nonprofit The Open Door (opendoorsdi.org) which he established prior to his death.

Marie Christian Norrisey was the editor of "The Open Door" bulletin since its first publication in 1969. She also worked with Msgr. Michael on each of his books, being co-author on two. A housewife and mother, she was an alumnus of Wilke College, formerly Bucknell University Junior College, in Pennsylvania. She was widely read in Jungian psychology and theology and became an instructor and administrator in the Spiritual Direction Institute, which Msgr. Chet launched in 1989 to train individuals in supporting others on their spiritual journeys. Mrs. Norrisey was a dedicated community volunteer and active in local and diocesan church organizations all of her adult life. She passed away in 2013.

Made in the USA
Coppell, TX
09 January 2025

44180821R00177